Working with Autobiographical Memories in Therapy

Aggregating 46 years of research, this book proposes a fresh approach on how to conduct assessment and therapy using autobiographical memories. It offers a system to identify and deconstruct major lifetime memories and shows how clinicians can work with the content of these memories to help clients better understand past events as present events are filtered through them.

Dr. Bruhn's first book on this subject, *Earliest Childhood Memories: Theory and Application to Clinical Practice* (1990), illustrated what could be learned about clients' present situation from the Early Memories Procedure (EMP), which is designed to identify and explore autobiographical memories of problematic experiences in therapy. The present book, which builds upon Dr. Bruhn's work with incarcerated women and male parolees, shows what can be done with these key memories by working directly on them in therapy. Dr. Bruhn showcases a new insight-oriented treatment paradigm, "memories work," to help resolve the issues identified in EMP responses. Chapters offer an alternative view of processing trauma and explore each facet of using memories work to design mental health interventions with clients. Included throughout are detailed case studies and techniques to re-engineer dysfunctional perceptions.

Clinicians and therapists will come away with the tools necessary to use memories work successfully with clients.

Arnold R. Bruhn, PhD, has more than 40 years of clinical experience in institutional and private practice settings. He developed memories work for individual and group psychotherapy, as well as the use of the Early Memories Procedure (EMP) and Cognitive-Perceptual (CP) therapy with individuals and groups. He has authored more than 20 journal articles, book chapters, and a book on autobiographical memory assessment techniques.

"In this book, Dr Bruhn provides an excellent synthesis of his 46 years of clinical work on the role of autobiographical memories in the treatment of psychological problems. This is an outstanding resource for clinicians who wish to understand how autobiographical memories can be incorporated into clinical practice and provides a wealth of profound insights

Working with Autobiographical Memories in Therapy
Assessment and Treatment

Arnold R. Bruhn

NEW YORK AND LONDON

First published 2020
by Routledge
52 Vanderbilt Avenue, New York, NY 10017

and by Routledge
2 Park Square, Milton Park, Abingdon, Oxon, OX14 4RN

Routledge is an imprint of the Taylor & Francis Group, an informa business

Description: New York, NY : Routledge, 2019. | Includes bibliographical
references and index.
Identifiers: LCCN 2019010057 (print) | LCCN 2019010603 (ebook) |
ISBN 9780429025716 (E-book) | ISBN 9780367132910 (hbk) | ISBN
9780367132927 (pbk) | ISBN 9780429025716 (ebk)
Subjects: | MESH: Mental Disorders—therapy | Memory, Episodic |
Psychotherapy | Personality Assessment
Classification: LCC RC489.W75 (ebook) | LCC RC489.W75 (print) | NLM
WM 460.5.M5 | DDC 616.89/1663—dc23
LC record available at https://lccn.loc.gov/2019010057

ISBN: 978-0-367-13291-0 (hbk)
ISBN: 978-0-367-13292-7 (pbk)
ISBN: 978-0-429-02571-6 (ebk)

Typeset in Sabon
by Swales & Willis Ltd, Exeter, Devon, UK

Contents

Statement of Purpose	vii
About the Author	ix
Abstract	x
Foreword by Henry J. Richards	xii
How Memories Work Began	xiv
Acknowledgments	xvi

An Introduction to Clinically Oriented
Autobiographical Memory   1

1   A Theory of Psychopathology Is Fundamental
to Psychotherapy   18

2   Analyzing Early Memories Is Like Learning a
New Language and a New Operating System   24

3   A Diagnostic System That Focuses on Where a Client
Is Stuck Helps Us Craft More Precise Interventions   27

4   When We Don't Understand a Client's Needs,
We Can Cause Damage   31

5   Bergson's Dilemma, or How Utility Actually Operates   36

6   Memories Are Programmed by the Mind   44

7   The Mind Affects the Body Even as the
Body Affects the Mind   50

vi *Contents*

8 Writing Memories Down Without Discussing
Them May Facilitate Understanding   53

9 "Instant Cures" in "Therapy"   58

Statement of Purpose

It is widely acknowledged in our language that personality evolves as experience accumulates. Else, how could we make credible statements like, "John was changed by the war" or "Pete became a different person after he married Carole"? Often, experience changes us. Some highly impactful experiences can be transformative. Another common observation is that we highlight powerful experiences in our memories via clarity, which preserves our account about what we have learned, whether that can be fully articulated or not. Many have described what we have learned as the narrative we create. Whatever your beliefs about a narrative, it is adaptive from an evolutionary perspective to remember and give priority to experiences that have moved you, either very positively or negatively. Strong affect signals that we have been especially impacted by that experience.

This book is organized around a central question: If an autobiographical memory is infused with both history and personality, how can we isolate and deconstruct what is related to personality; and how can that information be used most effectively to assess and treat clinical patients? To illustrate the assessment component, I cut and pasted the first part of Benjamin Franklin's autobiography (Bruhn, 2006) into an extended Part I of *The Early Memories Procedure* (EMP; Bruhn, 1989a) to illustrate how this method works even in memoirs. Many who read this book creatively will imagine powerful applications of this methodology. I offer in this book the concept of *load-bearing memories* (Chapter 9), which, when changed, almost instantly reorganize how other significant events are constructed. Load-bearing memories illustrate how perception, and ultimately personality, can be impacted when key elements in autobiographical memory are reconfigured.

How is it proposed that autobiographical memories be viewed? The latest recounting of an autobiographical memory reflects the most current comingling of history and personality, which in turn mirrors the most updated example of how we process important events in our lives. That version incorporates the template used to process experience and transforms it into what some call the narrative. Once we have described

viii *Statement of Purpose*

the template used to select, organize and interpret experience, we have the tool we need to assess and treat individuals who present with psychologically based emotional problems. I cannot overstate the importance of this template.

I will demonstrate in this book how various kinds of memories—

matic" will change forever.

Arnold R. Bruhn

About the Author

In 1972 Arnold R. Bruhn began working with early childhood memories and the assessment of autobiographical memories. In 1976 he accepted a position as an assistant professor of psychology at George Washington University and later a joint appointment with the George Washington University Medical School. At GW Dr. Bruhn founded the child and adolescent training track of the clinical psychology program and served at the same time as director of the Therapeutic Nursery and staff psychologist at Alexandria Community Mental Health Center, doing child and family work and training interns and externs. In 1982 he proposed the Cognitive-Perceptual theory of personality in conjunction with his work on autobiographical memories and has written about two dozen papers and book chapters on these subjects. His book, *Earliest Childhood Memories: Theory and Application to Clinical Practice* (Praeger, 1990), is the primary source for clinicians who want to learn to assess autobiographical memories.

Bruhn holds a PhD in clinical psychology from Duke University and interned at Duke Medical Center. He holds a certificate from the American Board of Assessment Psychology and is a fellow of the Society for Personality Assessment. He completed training in Imago Therapy. He finished a two-year postdoctoral course on the Millon system with the Institute for Advanced Studies in Personality and Psychopathology.

Bruhn developed an anger management program for the U.S. Parole and Probation Commission to treat aggressive parolees, and for five years he worked in a study for the National Institute of Drug Abuse to create and implement a model treatment program for multiply incarcerated women with substance-abuse-related crimes. The program reduced recidivism by 52%. Bruhn believes that working with memories provides an ideal opportunity to help clients resolve the effects of traumas and psychological wounds.

Arnold Bruhn maintains a private practice in Bethesda, Maryland and lectures on the assessment of autobiographical memory and how memories work can change us. He has offered workshops to numerous groups, including: The Society for Personality Assessment, the Maryland Psychological Association, and Patuxent Institution.

Abstract

offers a one-minute procedure to address a key assessment question that, heretofore, has not been answerable: Where are assessment clients stuck in their lives, and how can psychotherapy (memories work) help them progress? The results of a five-year, $2.5 million National Institute of Drug Abuse (NIDA) project[1] are summarized using *The Early Memories Procedure* (Bruhn, 1989a), insight-oriented memories work, and a therapeutic community condition focused on treating females multiply incarcerated for substance-abused-related crimes. The study found that the recidivism rate dropped by 52% among study participants using a 15-month post-release criterion period. This finding is unprecedented for previously reported insight-oriented therapy studies. Commonly rejected by prison inmates, insight-oriented therapy has historically been ineffective. Memories work was subsequently undertaken in a new treatment study with male parolees (mostly very dangerous) over approximately two years with similar results—less than 20% recidivism during the time subjects were in group.[2] The writer is also pleased to report that an enduring mystery regarding the operation of memory has been resolved. Henri Bergson observed over 100 years ago that the retention of memories conforms to the principle of utility. Bergson's argument was extended by reverse-engineering memories to depict how the mind operates on memory, which in turn enables us to observe how "utility" regulates the selection and depiction of events recalled. This method is disclosed in its entirety for the first time and its operation illustrated by clinical cases. The results from the NIDA prison study address its efficacy. The writer introduces a new insight-oriented treatment paradigm—*memories work*—to facilitate self-awareness and behavior change based on issues uncovered in the Early Memories Procedure assessments.

Notes

1 This research took place with the generous support of National Institute on Drug Abuse research grant, 5 RO1 DA09646-05, *Effective Addiction Treatments for Female Offenders*. Friends Research was the research group. Henry Richards was the PI. The perspective about the findings is mine.
2 The report was supported under *Treatment Services for Federal Defendants and Offenders*, Mental Health and Anger Management Services, Solicitation No. 0416-04-MHAPG. Paul Montalbano was the administrator and PI. Again, the interpretation of the findings is my own.

Foreword

treatment for traumatized and often personality-disordered women that had led therapists rushing down dead-ends, I contacted Arnold Bruhn and learned directly from the horse's mouth about the power of memory work in assessment and therapy. Bruhn was familiar to me by way of his articles and by his reputation in the Washington area as an effective therapist.

That was in 1987. A decade later, Bruhn's Early Memories Procedure (EMP)[1] was being used as the core component of an assessment-driven approach to the treatment of incarcerated female substance abusers. The program was developed with Bruhn's assistance as part of a federally funded research project for which I was the principal investigator. In another setting, the EMP was being used to intervene and manage male and female federal probationers and parolees who were referred for anger management treatment or to contain risk for dangerousness related to their mental illnesses. At Patuxent Institution, Maryland's historic treatment prison experiment, the EMP was being used as a core component in the sex-offender treatment program and as a means to structure individual psychotherapy with emotionally disturbed offenders.

More recently, I have continued to use the EMP to conduct forensic assessments and to structure and streamline individual treatment for diverse patients. When they use the EMP, therapists and evaluators find they, too, are getting the goods straight from the horse's mouth; that is, through their early memories patients tell us the perceptions and expectations that have been and remain of critical importance in their lives. Often hard-boiled offenders volunteer interpretations of their memories or energetically remark on their importance. Individuals who were aware that I may ultimately render professional opinions that are opposite of those they want have thanked me for the experience of collecting and interpreting their memories with the EMP. This happens because people intuit, or quickly catch on, that their memories contain, in embryo, both the content and structure of their lives—the attitudes and notions that guide them. Bruhn's method brilliantly captures the logic of the person–situation nexus, of the patient's propensity to self-select situations that perpetuate his or her problems. The EMP is artfully designed to gradually convert these intuitions into specific, actionable self-knowledge statements that are held with great confidence; they are inherently motivating because their clarity and precision undermine helplessness and the fear that one cannot change. With the EMP, therapists are able to provide patients with both the key understandings and the motivation they need to take responsibility for their own change process.

Henry J. Richards, PhD
Forensic Psychologist, Private Practice, Seattle, WA
Author, *Therapy of the Substance Abuse Syndromes* (1993)

Note

1 The EMP was used to understand and treat the trauma associated with the current incarceration via memories work. Dr. Richards's press release concerning the research interventions—memories work and Therapeutic Community—at the Women's Prison can be seen in Appendix B.

How Memories Work Began

were transacted. I collected data on such events, as required, but I did not hold this information in the same high regard as my supervisors did, who viewed this information as significant and "objective."

I also wanted to collect "early memories." What happened? I was permitted to collect them and was thought to be, I'm sure, "eccentric." My case was not helped, I'm certain, by my own struggles to advocate clearly and cogently for what I believed was a better practice. Yet I was as certain of my position as I would have been explaining where the sun rises in the summer sky.

Nearly 30 years later as I was attending a presentation featuring the Dalai Lama at Constitutional Hall in Washington, DC, the explanation finally came to me. An audience member asked the Dalai Lama to explain to us how his monks could be brutally tortured by their Chinese captors, even horribly burned, and not suffer trauma from being victimized. An amazing question! The Dalai Lama paused for a moment, then patiently explained: His monks had been trained in advance to pray for those who brutalized them, to forgive them even as they were suffering unimaginable pain. The purpose of this, the audience member persisted? Because, even in the case of death, the Dalai Lama explained, the chain of karma would be broken. There would be no need for soldier and monk to exchange places in successive lifetimes until each could experience the other's perspective with understanding and compassion. The learning cycle would be completed through the monks' suffering and forgiveness.

In the deathly stillness that followed the Dalai Lama's answer, I could finally explain my position in 1975. It wasn't the experience itself. It was how the experience was integrated within the mind, which could best be understood from the patient's memory of the experience, not from the objective experience itself.

What made that realization so compelling for me?

I already understood at a deeper level what the Dalai Lama explained to the audience. But words and an example eluded me. The Dalai Lama was sharing not only a spiritual perspective but a psychological axiom regarding traumas. An important key to self-healing is to understand and accept the motives of those who harm us. But how to do this? By beginning with the memory of the experience. And by understanding the perspective of the responsible agent without agreeing with it or endorsing it. That is why I wanted to obtain the memories of my clients and not just mark the developmental event. Once I "lived" my client's memories, I understood how my client understood himself and his world. And the seed of healing was thus germinated. Through compassion. Beginning with my own, then sharing it with the trauma victim. Whether either of us accepted reincarnation or not.

Sometimes answers to questions come only after many years of waiting for the right experience.

Acknowledgments

mental illnesses of the medical school model. Erickson's role was to help people get where they wanted to go in life but were unable to reach without assistance. Schiffman's chapter on Erickson (Schiffman, 1998) remains one of the most accessible dissections of Erickson's methods extant.

My parents, Arnold and Paula Bruhn, supplied me with enough memories to last a lifetime. My parents loved each other more than any two people had a right to expect, and they had an abundance left for me, their only child. From this experience I came to appreciate the immense importance of positive bonding. When a solid primary bond is formed, trust and security can follow, and, as I can see from my own memories, we accumulate the confidence to leave the nest and try life for ourselves. I thank them for providing the essentials!

My first wife, Arlene, patiently and skillfully typed the papers that became my thesis, my major area paper, and doctoral dissertation. I am grateful for her contribution and for her willingness to let me obsess over the hills in my intellectual world that only later became mountains. We begin where we must begin. Thank you!

My children, Alexis and Erika, suffered my intellectual odyssey with few complaints. More would have been acceptable. Thank you for putting up with my absences as I struggled to bring life to the ideas between these covers.

Ken Feigenbaum, my friend and longtime collaborator, has been a constant source of energy, questions, and support for more than 30 years.

Acknowledgments xvii

And, just as important, skepticism. His feedback has been much appreciated. I hope the journey has been as enjoyable for you as it has for me.

I gratefully acknowledge comments from Steven Finn, Marv Acklin, Henry Jay Richards, and Brenda Calfee on earlier versions of this book. Louise Straight helped with the editing and provided a sounding board. Thank you all!

Arnold R. Bruhn

An Introduction to Clinically Oriented Autobiographical Memory

Nobel prize winning philosopher, Henri Bergson (2004) once commented about the operation of memory: "If there be memory . . . it is with a view of utility . . . The [mind chooses]. . . the useful memory, that . . . may . . . illuminate the present situation with a view to ultimate action." As the Bergson comment anticipates, two questions about autobiographical memory have become foundational to the emerging field of *clinically oriented autobiographical memory*: "What makes us recall the memories we do?" and "What makes us recall what we do in the way that we do?" These questions have vexed great minds over the millennia.[1] Bergson, a Nobel Prize-winning philosopher, has offered his perspective, which provides a place to begin. Herein I address these questions, which energize personality.[2] If we can answer them, we will have progressed considerably toward a general theory of personality.[3] Part of the core of the book will explain in what ways this information is useful. To paraphrase Bergson, we remember what we do for a reason, and utility is the primary regulator. The same process that selects and shapes autobiographical memories impacts personality; the "gears" that operate on the first exert a partly determinative effect upon the second, and that observation provides yet another compelling reason for addressing these questions.

When this work began 46 years ago, what was the field of autobiographical memory like? Adlerians were interested only in the earliest recollection as it was believed to best convey the style of life and something about its probable etiology. Those who are interested in exploring Adler's approach to early recollections and clinical problems are referred to his 1929 classic, *The case of Miss R.*

Scattered psychologists acknowledged the earliest memory as having a narrow use in personality assessments, often related to reconstructing a client's early developmental eras. Freudians were not particularly interested in assessment as a distinct clinical discipline. They focused on treatment and tended to use assessments narrowly—for example, is Patient X a good candidate for analytic treatment? They were uninterested in readily recalled early memories; they wanted to bring repressed memories to consciousness and while doing so liberate psychic energy that it might be deployed for other activities—love and work. No one in

2 Introduction

the early 1970s was interested in other early memories or in memories from later eras for personality assessment.

By 1982 my work with memories had begun to attract some attention, and I was invited to participate in the largest multi-site, multi-method treatment of depression ever attempted, which was headquartered at

autobiographical memories—even so much as a test sample—from my patients. The PI had elected to go with Beck's Inventory and other procedures to assess patients—all quite respectable—and memories were not invited to our research paradigm even as silent observers. As I was to learn, mainstream psychiatry, not just our PI, did not have warm, fuzzy feelings about memories and their role in psychiatric syndromes—either as correlates or determinants. That experience forced a detour in my approach which, I am certain, would have led to the same major gains in how we treat depression that I had already observed in my private practice patients. Unfortunately, I had to wait until 1995 to obtain a memory research sample, and then with treatment outcome results I still find shocking (see Chapter 11).

My plan with memories, as it evolved, involved the following: determine how best to assess autobiographical memory (orally or in writing), assess the whole of it (not just early memories), identify the often unknown problems that culminated in a client's requesting therapy, and develop a therapy plan to resolve the problems identified in the assessment via memories work. In 1972 *traumatic* memories in particular were not solicited in assessment by any school of psychotherapy. Fast forward to the middle 1980s when the Early Memories Procedure (EMP) was actively in construction. What became the EMP included the earliest memory, four mostly early memories linked by association to the first, the clearest/most important memory of the lifetime (all spontaneous memories), and 15 directed memories of different types—e.g., school, punishment, mother. Use of the EMP in 1989 was the first time autobiographical memories were proposed to explore and articulate the personality—for me it was like a rocket into

Introduction 3

space. Incredibly exciting! My 1990 book, which introduced the EMP, was the first non-edited book on early memories and introduced the clinically oriented field of autobiographical memory *de novo*. The notion of probing for childhood molestations and traumas via an assessment of autobiographical memory was previously unknown. Nor had there been any discussion about preserving the "forensic integrity" of the memory itself, as I (Bruhn, 1995a) pointed out in a chapter that, in part, demonstrated how to assess the memories of molestation victims. I developed memories work as a distinct method of psychotherapy beginning in 1985, and the first refereed study of its efficacy was published in 1997 (DeMuth & Bruhn) with a sample of prison inmates.

The full development of the field thus required the following: Procedures to assess, a method to analyze memories, and a plan to resolve the issues identified. The clinical use of autobiographical memories required an elaboration and articulation of Bergson's original thinking.

Bergson proposed that memory follows the principle of utility. The next step? The content of memory follows the same principle; similarly for the earliest memory and for memories connected by association to the earliest memory. When we move to the level of understanding, however, everything becomes less clear. What makes the earliest memory useful? Useful how?

We might suppose Bergson's insight was partly based on an intuitive grasp of how memory functions across a wide variety of situations. Memory, we understand, is not designed to collect information, such as nonsense syllables, that has no obvious purposeful use—not now, not ever. Synthesized, Bergson's quandary is obvious: The principle of utility provides an overarching explanation for how memory operates—save the wheat, discard the chaff—but at the next level of analysis memory function remains unknown. What is the next level? Not just how memory operates but how individual memories function. What parameters guide their selection and organization?

To move forward, I gambled on an approach I intuited, namely to reverse-engineer specific memories as if they were mechanical objects, to better understand how they were constructed and what their design said about memory. Unfortunately, there were no tools and methods of analysis to make the process easier and consistent. A scientific process requires reliability for psychological processes—independent labs must be able to replicate the original result. We will introduce those tools and methods (Chapter 5) and illustrate their use so we can explain how memories work (see Chapters 9, 11) can be used with deliberate intent to alter the personality, as opposed to how we traditionally practice insight-oriented therapy. Memories work, as is true with any insight-oriented therapy, values and encourages insight and self-awareness, but it does not end there. With memories work, cognitive and personality changes also commonly take place fairly early in therapy—clients no longer perceive the world as they did before. How do we know that?

4   Introduction

Clients tell us so, but more importantly, they no longer *behave* the same in critical situations. For them the world has changed, people are seen differently, they see themselves differently, and their behavior adjusts to these new perceptions.

In addition to utility, an important developmental process impacts

conclusively demonstrated. In the autobiographical memory literature, over 100 years ago survey studies demonstrated that people of different ages recalled qualitatively different events. For instance, in a wide-ranging chapter, "Individual Memories," published the same year as Freud's classic work (1899/1913) on dreams, Colegrove (1899) reported memories from 1,658 subjects, including 1,372 from Whites, 182 from African Americans, and 104 from American Indians; his sample included subjects of widely varying ages and reported memories even from persons 80 years old and beyond. His chapter reproduces an early memory questionnaire (14 items), including some thought-provoking matters that, over a century later, have never been adequately researched—for example, a section on "false memories" that anticipates the False Memory Syndrome controversy in the United States by over 90 years (see Loftus & Ketcham, 1994).[5] Had psychologists in the 1990s read Colegrove's paper, it is interesting to speculate how this scandal might have played out differently.

It is difficult for me even to imagine personality without a robust contribution from autobiographical memories. How can we know ourselves as individuals without a reservoir of memories and life experiences to draw from? Ultimately, the self is built from what we have done, what we have experienced, critical events in our lives, the relationships we have built, our triumphs and our setbacks. Long story short: We draw heavily, consciously or otherwise, upon our memories, which preserve our most relevant life experiences. And the principle of utility, as Bergson posited, regulates the selection.

Introduction 5

At birth, the infant is more *latent* personality than personality shaped by his memories. With time and exposure to the world come life experiences. As they aggregate and assume form and structure, memories reflect and express the personality. With experience, personality and memories interact. If we recall mostly good experiences, our mood tilts in that direction; similarly with negative experiences, which produce a more melancholy, less hopeful personality. And thus, experience, and how we construct that experience, begins to influence mood and personality and create many response tendencies. Kandel's inquiry (2006) into the biology of learning provides a brain-oriented perspective on these concepts.

A general theory of personality must describe those aspects of personality that make us different as individuals. Much comes into play: what we have learned, and how we learned it; how compassionate we are, and how we came to be that way; what we feel and how we express those feelings; what interests we have; what needs are important to us as individuals; and so forth.

And, of course, we attempt to describe aspects of personality that have interest to us, via ink blots, storytelling, intelligence testing, projective assessments, pencil-and-paper tests, diagnostic procedures, and so forth. Each method permits an aspect of personality to be depicted, as shaped and influenced by the device used. The responses to these instruments, it hardly needs to be stated, are influenced if not determined by a store of life experiences preserved and organized in autobiographical memory

Rather than describe a general theory of personality at this time, I will focus on memory questions that bear on how autobiographical memory operates. Such questions seem deceptively simple, yet they are not always easy to answer. To begin, I sketched out existing approaches to autobiographical memory, which focus on the recall of specific events from our lives ("I remember one time . . .") that have a beginning, a middle, and an end. That process culminated in a brief review of existing theoretical perspectives (Bruhn & Last, 1982)—Freudian, ego-psychological, and Adlerian. Having sketched out the beginnings of Cognitive-Perceptual (CP) theory in that paper as a fourth approach (see Table 0.1), I elaborated that model several years later (Bruhn 1990a, b). CP theory reminds us, simply, that as we accumulate life experiences, we make inferences about who we are, what the world is like, and what we can expect from our interactions with others. This material is sampled by memories in the EMP and is available for analysis, much as blood analyzed in a physician's lab test can be used to provide data suggestive of physical illnesses or their absence. These beliefs and expectations now begin to influence how we interpret subsequent life experiences—put simply, once we form certain core opinions, what we experience subsequently is shaped and reinforced by those opinions. Thus, the basis for the expression, "Been there, done that." What evolutionary benefit is there to learn and relearn the same lesson as if we have never had that experience?

6 Introduction

Table 0.1 Four EM Models

---

1 Freudian: Classical psychoanalysis
   Selected references: Freud (1899/1913, 1917/1955)
2 Adlerian: School of individual psychology
   Selected references: Adler (1912/1917, 1927, 1929, 1931, 1937);

ing several of his own memories [see pp. 113–124 for an illustration]. If the goal is to know yourself better, Estrade's method makes sense—that is also the goal of Freud's psychoanalytic method.

Alfred Adler's view of memories is close to my own. Adler emphasized that we recall what is useful:

> Thus his memories represent his "Story of My Life"; a story he repeats to himself to warn him or comfort him, to keep him concentrated on his goal, and to prepare him, by means of past experiences, so that he meets the future with an already tested style of action.
>
> (Ansbacher & Ansbacher, 1956, p. 351)

Notice how Adler focused on process—this is what memories do and here is how we use them. Adler thus walks us down a path similar to Bergson's, with its emphasis on utility. The cognitive-perceptual approach, however, offers a more nuanced perspective on the role and function of autobiographical memories as it differentiates, for example, between positive and negative affect memories, extremely clear and less clear memories, spontaneous and directed memories, and what each tells us about a memory and its role in autobiographical memory.

A not unrelated question regarding memory and remembering is what makes us forget. From Bergson's perspective, forgetting implies a sloughing off of matters that have less importance—that is, less utility—the inverse of what causes events to be recalled. Early in my career I worked intensively with a man who had a hostile relationship with his mother,

Introduction 7

who favored his twin and scapegoated my client. As we made progress on this issue, a memory of his mother grilling and berating him at the kitchen table under what he remembered as a metaphoric bare lightbulb began to fade.

Remnants of those feelings remained, however, which occasioned me to remind him of being emotionally battered for doing something trivial that he had already admitted to and, as she continued to berate him, taking full responsibility to stop the abuse. I called this memory back on a fair number of occasions, so he could reconnect with the experience quickly while reducing his painful reaction to it, but he now, to my shock, he denied his memory entirely. He looked squarely at me and said he believed I was confusing him with someone else—another client perhaps? His reaction unsettled me. Was I wrong?

The next session I pulled out his EMP and showed him the memory. His astonishment was palpable. Even while rereading this memory, which he inscribed in the EMP in his own hand, he stated he could not recall the incident in question. I must emphasize that this man had a fabulous memory and excelled in a profession where an excellent memory is a bedrock necessity for success. I pointed out the progress he had made, clearly so much that he could not even recall the incident. And he had. His relationships with women had improved tremendously, as had his relationship with his mother. He then completed a new EMP which included a new set of memories that dealt with emerging self-concept issues. As abusive mother exited stage left, he was left to reimagine who he was post abusive mother.

As progress is made, new memories become ascendant, and a new EMP needs to be completed.[6] As he continued to progress, the client subsequently redid his EMP a third time, and new issues once again emerged.

We must also reassess the essential nature of a memory itself. I have argued from early in my career that memories are not eidetic representations of the original event. I believe that today. While I believe my father appeared to have a photographic memory,[7] I also believe few mortals do unless we train ourselves, like Jerry Lucas, to memorize 50 pages of a telephone book (see Wikipedia). As to early memories specifically, if early memories are not photographically accurate, what are they exactly? Cognitive-perceptual theory holds that "recollections of one's early life are particularly susceptible to . . . [overwriting from subsequent experience] as each major lesson extracted from life's experiences can be processed and superimposed upon the corpus of one's EMs" (Bruhn 1995a, p. 281). Few of us have photographically accurate memories.[8] Most of us have preserved a recollection of an early event that is overwritten and contaminated by subsequent events and later understandings. Such is true of later life memories as well. As time passes, memories can change. This is why—if factual accuracy is the goal—we need to write the memory down or videotape our remembrance as soon as possible

8   *Introduction*

after the event in question. We may have misperceived what we thought we saw, as Loftus's (1994) eyewitness research demonstrates, but at least we will have an accurate record of what we believed we saw at the time.

Autobiographical memories can also be used for model building to deconstruct variables of interest. Early memories have been used to

1993a), and I will return to it here. Table 0.2 is intended to be selective, not exhaustive, and includes highlights from the past 125 years. Theiler (2009), one of my dissertation students, offers a much more detailed compendium that is well worth reviewing.

Table 0.2 Selected Noteworthy Autobiographical Publications During the Past 125 Years

1890	William James. The formation of memories is dependent upon perception. What we don't perceive we don't remember. James commented thusly about the selectivity of perception: "Millions of items of the outward order are present in my senses which never properly enter into my experience. Why? Because they have no interest for me . . ." Interests, then, organize and determine perception.
1890s	Several pioneering papers on EMs: Miles (1893); Henri & Henri (1898).
1899	Colegrove. First attempt to study early memories by age of the person recollecting. Does subject matter of early memories differ by the age of the recollector?
1899	Freud: *The interpretation of dreams*. Introduction of psychoanalysis. Primary focus of analysis: To use dreams to uncover fragments of "repressed" memories and thereby to free up energy previously used to maintain repression. Freudian theory as an energetically oriented mechanistic meta psychological theory.

1917	Freud: Analysis of the first EM of Johann Goethe, German dramatist, poet, and scientist.
1912–1937	Adler: Classic contributions to EMs, including an excellent but little-known case study, *The case of Miss R* (1929).
1932	Bartlett: *Remembering: A study in experimental and social psychology.* A classic book that argued for the concept of memories as constructions versus veridical reproductions. Argued the recalled event is "a construction, largely made up [of an attitude and its general effect that is] that of a justification of the attitude" (p. 207). Mechanically, the "attitude" justifies the facts of the memory, which helps explain how it is that so many facts in memories are not accurate.
1948	Waldfogel: Monograph and first partial review of the literature.
1956	Ansbacher & Ansbacher. Thorough organization of Alfred Adler's theoretical writing and his views on Early Recollections (ERs).
1961	Langs & Reiser: A psychoanalytically based EM scoring system.
1968	Mayman: Presidential address to the Society for Personality Assessment on EMs. Papers in the early 1970s relating to an object relations-based EM scoring system. See also 1984.
1976	Bruhn. What explains individual process in perception? Perception is not commonly photographic so there appears to be "a perception-memory-perception feedback loop in which 'attitudes' tend to remain constant until the individual is confronted with a novel experience . . . having sufficient impact that the pre-suppositions which control the selectivity of the perceptual process are called into question" (p. 4).
1978–present	Neisser: His work with long-term autobiographical memory as fact and history, especially *Memory observed: Remembering in natural contexts* (1982), diverges from my own. His goal: To eliminate personality from long-term autobiographical memories while focusing on "pure history."
1979	Olson (editor): The first book on EMs—a collection of classic EM papers and some new ones, mostly by Adlerians.
1982	Binder & Smokler: How EMs can be used to focus psychotherapy.
1982	Bruhn & Last: A review of four EM models. The Cognitive-Perceptual (CP) model introduced. Book (Bruhn, 1990b) offers a more complete version.
1982	Bruhn & Schiffman: An analysis of attitudes that weave together and sustain an attitude of personal control/responsibility using first memory data as sources.
1983	Last: The Comprehensive Early Memories Scoring System (CEMSS) introduced.
1984	Bruhn: Review of EM field, the first since Waldfogel. Emphasizes clinical applications.

(continued)

Table 0.2 (continued)

1984	Bruhn & Bellow: First memory of Dwight David Eisenhower. Introduces application of CP method to EMs and compares interpretations with those from other models. CP model: "The individual's needs, fears, interests and major beliefs constitute
	perceive and remember. . . . [T]o treat depression by correcting thinking errors is like trying to eliminate dandelions by chopping off their tops but ignoring their roots" (p. 595). "[E]arly memories provide . . . perhaps the most direct approach to assessing how an individual constructs his world" (p. 596).
1986	Rubin: *Autobiographical memory*. In the tradition of Neisser (the basic science of long-term autobiographical memory, not clinically oriented).
1987	Bruhn & Bellow: The Cognitive-Perceptual approach to the interpretation of early memories: The earliest memories of Golda Meier. Golda Meir's early memories interpreted using CP model. See also the first memories of Eisenhower, 1984, first publication on interpreting a series of EMs using the CP method.
1989	Bruhn: *The Early Memories Procedure* (EMP) published. First procedure to assess a set of spontaneous EMs (Part I) and the whole of autobiographical memory.
1989	Bruhn: *Romantic relationships procedure* (RRP) published. Assesses most important romantic relationships through memories of those relationships. Focus: What makes romantic relationships work or fail.
1990	Davidow & Bruhn: Replicates earlier results from Bruhn & Davidow (1983), which demonstrated how delinquents and non-delinquents could be distinguished via EM data. The first formal attempt to identify sociopathic elements in EMs. Confirms several observations by Alfred Adler, particularly regarding the frequent appearance of rule breaking in the early memories of delinquents.

1990	Bruhn: The first non-edited book on applied autobiographical memory and how to assess it. Method illustrated in a complete EMP, which is interpreted stepwise.
1990	Bruhn: *Journal of Personality Assessment* paper introduces CP theory as a personality theory focused on memory and its operation. CP is a contextual meta-theory (Pepper, 1942), not a mechanistic theory (Freud and psychoanalysis). CP theory is designed to describe the context that guides and directs perception in its role of presenting a coherent worldview. In the first textbook of psychology, William James (1890) observed about the selectivity of perception: "Only those items which I notice change my mind—without selective interest, experience is utter chaos. Interest alone . . . gives . . . intelligible perspective, in a word" (p. 402). Just as perception is directed by interests, so also can we assert with remembering. As Bartlett (1932) noted: "The past is being continually remade, reconstructed in the interests of the present . . ." CP theory can be reduced to ten key propositions that clarify how personality functions in memory. Bruhn argues: It can be asserted that "autobiographical memory is absolutely basic and essential to any conceptualization of personality grounded in self psychology" (p. 95). Put another way, we say "history" when we mean "fact" and "truth," but "history" reduces to "his-story," which is our individual construction of "the truth." With apologies to Neisser, the "story" in "his-story" is just as likely, all things considered, to reflect the individual's current personality organization than it is "fact" and objective "truth."
1991	Last & Bruhn: The CEMSS expanded (CEMSS-R) to include content and process themes (Section VII). These themes identify the psychological structures common in our Western culture that filter how we process current experience.
1991	Ross: *Remembering the personal past*. A compendium of material pertinent to applied autobiographical memory from an analytic perspective.
1992	Bruhn: Two papers in the *Journal of Personality Assessment* introduce the EMP as the first projective test of autobiographical memory and interpret a sample EMP.
1992	Tobey & Bruhn: Distinguishing dangerous from non-dangerous chronic psychiatric patients via EMs with a false-positive rate of 6%. Provides specific guidance as to how dangerous individuals differ in their recollections from non-violence prone subjects. "In its 73% classification of dangerous and nondangerous patients, the EMAPSS [Early Memories Aggressiveness Potential Score System] fared respectably

(continued)

Table 0.2 (continued)

in comparison with studies cited in the literature . . . The EMAPSS false-positive rate was an impressively low 6%, with only one patient misidentified as dangerous. . . . It thus appears that the presence of aggression on the EMAPSS is pertinent memories.

1995	Bruhn: Ideographic aspects of injury memories: Applying contextual theory to the Comprehensive Early Memories Scoring System—Revised. Analyzes ideographic aspects of the most common content theme (sickness, injury or hospitalization) in the spontaneous EMs of outpatient mental health subjects. Also reports the prevalence of content and process themes from an outpatient clinical sample.
1995	Kotre: *White gloves: How we create ourselves through memory.* Memory formation. Strength of book: What memories are not. See also Notes, pp. 247–268.
1995	Bruhn: Early memories in personality assessment. An updated overview of applied autobiographical memory. Includes the EMP of a man who had been sexually abused as a boy scout in a massive New England molestation involving upwards of 100 victims.
1995–2002	Richards & Bruhn: NIDA treatment study of hundreds of women multiply incarcerated for substance-abuse-related crimes. Treated with TC and memories work. Recidivism reduced by 52%. Following study with violent male parolees who received anger management plus memories work. Fewer than 20% recidivated during group. Results discussed in Chapter 11.
2000	Howe: *The fate of early memories.* Excellent basic science discussion of autobiographical memory.

2006	Bruhn: In celebration of his 300th birthday: Benjamin Franklin's Early Memories Procedure. With Franklin's *Autobiography* as source material, the paper illustrates how one can approximate Part I of the EMP and thereby undertake a psychological study of an historical figure using just EMs. A more limited memory sample was used previously by Bruhn with President Eisenhower, President Nixon, Golda Meir, John Muir, Gandhi and others serving as examples of how personal issues and needs are reflected in important memories. These papers illustrate how techniques borrowed from applied autobiographical memory can be used to study the personalities of historical figures.
2006	Kandel: *In search of memory*. Nobel-winning scientist offers an overview of learning and memory at a cellular level. Extraordinary book!
2006	Karson: *Using early memories in psychotherapy*. Karson "treat(s) early memories as literature" (p. 3), an approach broadly consistent with CP and Adlerian approaches which view memories as "stories" about "life"—who I am and how the world operates.
2008	Estrade: *You are what you remember*. Popular press psychoanalytically based book on how to understand early memories and what they mean. Grounded on analytic theory. Relies on free associations to uncover hidden meanings in memories.
2009	Theiler: *Early memories: Theory, research, and practice: Accessing essential meaning in counseling*. Well researched.
2015	Bruhn: The Early Memories Procedure and its origins. During the 1980s and early 1990s I used different methods to assess autobiographical memory. This chapter deals with that history and how my thinking evolved as I moved from assessment to developing memories work to resolve the problems that were identified. The present book expands this material to introduce memories work as an insight-oriented therapy that focuses on changing perceptions and attitudes and, ultimately, personality.
2015	Mosak & Di Pietro: *Early recollections: Interpretative method and application*. Adlerian approach to early recollections. The first author is a pre-eminent Adlerian clinician and a master practitioner with early recollections. For a synthesis of Adlerian concepts, also see Ansbacher & Ansbacher (1956).

In this book I will review some of the more important ideas I have proposed in the past 46 years about autobiographical memory and personality. I could have focused my research solely on assessing auto-biographical memory, but once I began, I wondered, like a cat batting a ball of yarn, whether I might unwind the negative perceptions integral to

14 Introduction

those memories. That is, could I deconstruct memories in therapy to determine how they functioned as a template and change them *directly* once a better understanding of the presenting problem was reached?[9] I will share some thoughts on problems that we encounter as we attempt to help clients unstick themselves, which is, after all, what motivates many clients do not know. *The Early Memories Procedure* was designed to make this process easier by giving clients time to sort through their store of personal memories at the beginning of the therapy process and identify issues that are especially salient for them.

To make this discussion more concrete, consider a woman who offered this "Traumatic Memory" from her EMP (p. 22).

> . . . My father had followed me down the hallway [of her home], and I found him pushing me into his bedroom and locking the door behind him. I was made to lie down on the bed, and he undid some of my clothes. I do not know why I did not shout out or do something but I didn't. I was basically immobile while he felt over and in me . . . I heard the snap as he put on a condom. He was slow and it was painful. I don't know if he finished or just stopped, but it was over and I was relieved . . . I felt a daze at school the next day and for several days to follow.

Did she tell anyone about this incident? She reports this was the first time she ever told anyone (EMP, question 3, p. 30). This incident happened about 20 years previous, so we know one therapeutic task would be to help her *find her voice*—learn to talk about things that upset or concerned her. Another is *trust*. She notes (EMP, p.22) after reporting the memory that she had always put her father on "a pedestal" and admired him. With the completed EMP in hand the therapist is now bound to report this violation to CPS (Child Protective Services), which we can anticipate

Introduction 15

would be extremely hard for this client, who we know from her memory has a problem *asserting herself* and *setting boundaries*. Because this violation took place with her father, we suspect she might find an easier time working with a *female therapist.* Could we figure all this out without her completed EMP? Most of it, given enough time, I suspect so. But considering how many memories she described before she reported the rape scene, it may have taken years of therapy, and how many other kids might her father have harmed before then?

As can be seen from this brief example, applied autobiographical memories have profound, game-changing implications for both assessment and psychotherapy.

If I may be pardoned for saying the obvious, some of the material in this book may "trigger" readers who have had similar experiences. This would include flashbacks, nightmares, uncomfortable feelings and the like. Those of you who have not confided in someone like a therapist before and integrated experiences like these may want to consider therapy for yourselves. Life happens. Sometimes unpleasantly. Various writers have reported that as many as two-thirds of women in prison (see Chapter 11) claim to have been sexually molested or raped as children or adolescents, and about 1% reported these experiences, in therapy or otherwise. Until very recently (2017) with the "Me Too" movement, women have not been encouraged to report experiences like this, and when they did, their reporting made it worse. Thankfully, our society appears to be changing its attitudes. Unfortunately, our current president has strongly asserted young men must be protected from false accusations, so it is difficult to know as of this writing how our culture will respond. My hope is that autobiographical memory exploration tools like the EMP will facilitate a process of healing.

To simplify, I have divided the book into chapter topics that the reader will hopefully find easy to navigate.

Notes

1 No one has suggested a satisfactory answer to these questions which, jointly, constitute a great conundrum in psychology. I have worked on them piecemeal before (see, for example, Bruhn, 1990a, 1990b; 1992a, 1992b). In this book I offer the most complete answer I have attempted.
2 When few autobiographical memories can be retrieved, personality appears to be largely "lost," as is evident with later stage Alzheimer's patients.
3 A general theory of personality can be conceptualized as addressing the question, "Who are we mentally and emotionally as psychological beings, and how did we become that way?" Autobiographical memories play a vital role in shaping that answer because they reveal what is important to us while simultaneously influencing our perceptions. Of course, there are other causative contributors such as genetics, family history, early learning, and so forth. These matters are not addressed here.
4 Around 1972 I began asking my older daughter—and her friends—about their earliest memory. She was two years old at the time. Children that age respond

16 Introduction

to the question as if they had been asked, "Tell me about *a* memory you have" or "Tell me about something that happened once." They do not understand *earliest* the way older children and adults do, as the word requires a mastery of temporal sequence. Around age seven, and even earlier for very intelligent children, most children begin to understand what *earliest* means and describe events that happened a year ago, or more, or even, in some cases, events that

however that opinion might be gussied up—with considerable damage to their credibility. For the legal profession, Bergson's principle of utility has largely been ignored with resulting damage to how we conduct witness interviews, just to touch upon one troubling area. Were I to be asked to consult to attorneys, I would recommend that witnesses write down and videotape their recollections of fact testimony, which is likely to degrade in the months and years ahead of trial unless something from that witness experience has touched them deeply. But even if it has, that material might still become reorganized and at least partly irretrievable.

7 In the 1930s the navy tested its men for typing ability and a photographic memory. According to his sister, my father was found to have the best score in the navy in the years preceding World War II. He was deployed to the American embassy in Germany to memorize a top-secret document roughly 60 pages in length that had to be typed from memory, perfectly, on board his ship after his return from the embassy. The material was so sensitive that no hard document could remain on his person for fear it might be stolen before he returned to his ship. The story from his sister was (I could not independently verify this) that he missed one punctuation mark in the 60 pages, which were otherwise accurate. I do not find this story remarkable—a good friend, for example, memorized three statistical texts down to the last comma, which I verified through testing him, for his final exam in statistics. My father's memory for daily events was similarly accurate, and I can recall his spontaneously reciting dramatic pieces he memorized as an actor in high school 50 years previous. My point? We can develop extremely accurate memories if properly motivated and trained, but examples like this stand out like blind Homer reciting classic epic poems to his audiences. They reflect a human potential, but they are not the norm.

8 This book focuses mostly on what memories mean and how they can be used in assessment and therapy. Kotre (1995) has written a unique book on memory formation that is worth perusing. Consider the following task: Watch a week's worth of video surveillance from a local store. Said Kotre: "Very little of that

Introduction 17

168 hours [of surveillance] would stay with you because very little would be worth remembering. But you'd get a good idea of what is potentially available to memory, and how boring most of it is" (p. 40). If I can put it this way, the residue of the residue of the residue is what we are interested in as we do memories work. In Kotre's terms: our scattered autobiographical memories are what remain after 100,000 hours of our personal surveillance tapes have been reviewed and the highlights have been extracted.

9 As a student and early career psychologist, I was strongly warned by several supervisors not to work with traumatic memories directly, as a psychosis might result. What I was told was the then consensus opinion. These warnings had the desired effect of making me extremely cautious at least as if I were deconstructing a pipe bomb in the dark. In my subsequent professional work, I found there is in fact a miniscule risk of triggering a psychosis. Of the clients I have treated in my career (perhaps 2,000), one did become psychotic when we focused on a memory in which she was abused. It turned out she had identified with her abuser and acted out as an adult what she experienced on a child. I suspect what caused the psychosis was the confluent experience of herself as victim, and the pain she experienced, superimposed on the adult memory of herself as abuser, which initially gave her a feeling of power but now caused her horrific pain and regret as she faced her own victimization. Once we worked on the nexus of the feelings, the psychosis began to dissipate, and she recovered uneventfully. The key to helping her, I believe, was to hear what happened with a much higher measure of empathy than the level she accorded to herself in memories work group. Compassion was the key to bridging this disparate set of experiences, one as victim, the other as victimizer.

1 A Theory of Psychopathology Is Fundamental to Psychotherapy

preschoolers, children, and adolescents meet criteria for various psychological problems. Millon (2006) used a conceptual approach similar to Achenbach's but began with *DSM* entities and over 100 behaviorally or cognitively oriented statements that adult respondents agree with or deny. Unfortunately, disease entities arise and disappear periodically in succeeding editions of the *DSM*, often not solely for scientific reasons, which can lead to professionally embarrassing discussions later—for example the description of homosexuality as a personality disorder (i.e., a "sickness" or disease), which was later disavowed, and similarly with personality disorders as a group in later revisions. Behaviorists demonstrate that behaviors can be shaped with various reinforcement schedules. Analysts describe hypothesized disorders as being caused by traumas, usually repressed, that occur at psychologically vulnerable psychosexual periods of development.

There is little consensus within our profession about what we treat, or should treat, in therapy, or how we can help individuals who present themselves for psychotherapy and what they suffer from. For instance, are clients "ill"? Are they suffering from repressed memories? Are they behaviorally defective or deficient in some way? Are they missing social skill sets or important life experiences? Or perhaps they have been adversely impacted by dysfunctional family systems? And when we assess a client, what do we need to look at? Behaviors, family systems, clinically significant patterns of behavior, or clusters of hallmarks that might meet certain *DSM* criteria while we rule out competing *DSM* entities?

Cognitive-perceptual (CP) theory (Bruhn, 1985; Bruhn, 1990a, b; Bruhn, 1995a; Bruhn & Bellow, 1987; Bruhn & Last, 1982) offers yet another approach to conceptualize what we do as therapists—for example, change attitudes and perceptions, add skill sets, change expectations and behaviors, work through traumas evident in memories, modify a maladaptive family system (with the family as a unit or with selected family members), and so forth. The primary goal is to *determine from the client's autobiographical memories what is causing the client to be stuck in dysfunctional patterns now and to develop a treatment strategy that will provide leverage to help the client to become unstuck and continue moving on in life.*

As CP theory views it, autobiographical memories help us understand what needs to be worked through and modified. Memories work is an active, strategic therapy. Those who do memories work understand that clients know at least preconsciously what is problematic; that their memories frame the problem and hint at a solution; and that the therapist is there to give voice to what is in the memory/perceptograph and help the client resolve the issue. Oddly, the therapist becomes a sort of memory translator.

On the other hand, analysts wait until repressed memories emerge, often through dreams; they assert energy then becomes freed up and available for other purposes. Insight-oriented therapists wait for the client to bring up critical memories and until then get to know the client better and establish rapport; meanwhile they work on the presenting problem, such as depression. Unfortunately, clients often neglect to disclose critical memories, such as sexual assaults, which means that therapy never addresses the most important reason the client sought therapy in the first place. A contrast to such approaches was one that assumed that certain repressed memories existed on the basis of clinical presentation and family of origin information. Such therapists—repressed memories clinicians—began probing for certain kinds of memories: "Your depression makes me think that you have been incested. What memories do you have of . . .?" This approach has been widely condemned. This method can culminate in creating memories that never occurred—so-called *false memories.*

The *Early Memories Procedure* (EMP; Bruhn, 1989a) bypasses the therapist and enables the client to explore his or her own internal process through a technique some have described as memory journaling (see Plate 1; *Romantic Relationships Procedure* was published the same year (1989b), see Plate 2). Its intentional "tell me more" process enables clients to connect with what is most affecting their lives at the beginning of therapy, when a minimal level of self-awareness can make the difference between committing to a therapy process and stopping before anything helpful takes place.

Bruhn's (1990b) intent was to create a procedure in the EMP that would permit an initial exploration of autobiographical memory. This was a daunting task which consumed about four years field testing several versions while the writer begged the indulgence of family, friends and clients. This process was conceptualized as following a journaling tradition which would invite a client to participate in an initial process of self-discovery and self-awareness. The goal was to create a device

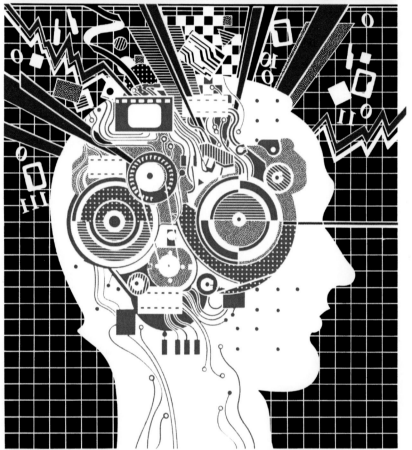

Plate 1 Cover of *The Early Memories Procedure*

Plate 2 Cover of *Romantic Relationships Procedure*
Source: Diane Bogardus

20 *A Theory of Psychopathology*

that facilitated self-awareness and insight. The publication that followed (Bruhn 1990a) also introduced the new personality theory—CP theory—that explained how personality could be observed from the vantage of autobiographical memory.

Many years previous, Adler (Ansbacher & Ansbacher, 1956) introduced the process of asking for the client's earliest recollection in the initial therapy visit: not the first memory when a client was incested or brutalized, but simply the first memory recalled. To my knowledge, no one ever sued Adler, or anyone in his group, for any problem related to this inquiry (in contrast to false memory practitioners for instance), which simply requests the "earliest recollection." By 1974 (see also Bruhn, 1976, Bruhn & Schiffman, 1982), I was asking for the first two early memories for comparisons in research on locus-of-control beliefs. As I began to supervise dissertation students (e.g., Bruhn & Davidow, 1983) at George Washington University, we worked with the four earliest memories.[1] By the late 1980s, as I worked with new therapy clients, I developed the EMP, which requested five memories, or four memories that were activated by association with the earliest, and the clearest or most important memory of a lifetime[2] (Memory 6). Integral to Part I of the EMP were various rating scales and several fill-in-the-blank questions, such as, "Which memory is your most important?" All memories in Part I are *spontaneous* memories (mostly the earliest and others by association). In Part II, I asked for 15 memories that often have clinical relevance which might have left out of Part I: The first memory of school, first punishment memory, first memory of mother, of father, the most traumatic memory, a memory of the parents involving substances or alcohol, and so forth. All 15 memories are *directed* memories. All are memories *I* think may be important but may not be at all important to the client. The differences between spontaneous and directed memories, which are usually not psychologically equivalent, are discussed in Bruhn and Schiffman (1982a).

For example, I once worked with a young woman who reported a memory of an inappropriate sexual experience with her uncle (a directed memory) in Part II of the EMP. I followed up in session with a comment about betrayal, assuming that this memory by its very nature had to be traumatic. She quickly corrected me, noting that her uncle treated her far better than anyone else in her family. She did not regard these experiences as traumatic. Once we venture into *directed* memories, we as professionals may have a much different take on the experience than our clients. For her, these were extremely positive experiences in which she felt important and valued. When I as her therapist began to reframe her perspective, she let me know she thought I was way off the mark and my comments out of bounds. She wanted to treasure the memory as it was, and she firmly corrected me.

In the last three pages of the EMP clients are asked to pick a memory and interpret it as they see appropriate, then to comment on any connection between any memory described and what brought them to therapy.

As a set of memories is assembled, my secondary goal is to teach clients by experience about the insight-oriented therapy process as I also assess their level of insight, self-awareness, and ability to reflect and introspect. For the first time, an assessment of autobiographical memory is possible before therapy begins, and the entire process is undertaken in the client's own hand outside the therapy hour. Not only have I never been sued by a client in conjunction with inquiring about memories, most of my clients have learned about themselves by working with the procedure and have expressed good feelings about the experience. At some point the risk reduction arm of our profession may conclude that the EMP is an effective instrument to forestall potential lawsuits just as I have found it to be. Indisputably, the EMP documents that the clinician made a responsible inquiry into areas like trauma and sexual abuse, which historically have provided fertile grounds for litigation.

The EMP reveals in about 60 seconds the "real reason" why the client is in therapy. How? The rating scales (EMP, pp. 9 and 10) identify the clearest (optimally rated as 5) and most negative (commonly rated as a 1) memories in Part I. The clearest memory, when it is also negative in affect, conveys that the memory highlights a major unresolved issue for the client (it is, after all, a negative affect memory). It also stands out in the memory (it is clearest, or among the clearest, in Part I). The further questions (EMP, p. 11) provide an opportunity to validate hypotheses: Commonly the client will explain what it is about the memory identified as the clearest/most negative memory that makes it most important. The client will often discuss the reasons in some detail. Many books and papers (Bruhn, 1990a; 1992a, b; 1995a; 2006, in press; Richards, 1993, Appendix C) provide examples of how memories and EMPs are interpreted with the CP method.

A brief example is taken from Bruhn (1990b). Two memories are rated 1–5s (very negative, exceptionally clear) by the S (p. 136). The "most significant" memory is Memory 5 (p. 136). The memory follows. The client's older brother, then 12 years old, died of a ruptured appendix. What made this memory important to her? She states: "I think Memory 5 was the most significant memory to me because I felt my brother was the only person I could be close to and depend on and he was gone." What brings her to psychotherapy now? She is feeling very alone and does not have anyone in her life as she did when her brother was alive whom she can depend on as she did then. The issue? To develop and deepen meaningful relationships which will leave her feeling better connected. What aspects in a relationship? To feel secure with being in an emotionally intimate relationship and being dependent. We know the S was married, so we can assume the marriage is not providing enough of what is most important to her. The EMP provides the answer to the question, "What brings you in?" in about 60 seconds.

Consider a second excerpt, which is presented more fully in Bruhn (1995a). The referring therapist told me his client, the husband, needed

22   A Theory of Psychopathology

individual therapy after he became romantically involved with a younger woman. His wife felt threatened, she had never been interested in sex, and the marriage disintegrated. The client agreed to complete an EMP, so I could get a clearer idea of his history. On p. 11 of the EMP, Memory 2 in Part I was listed as his "most significant," which was also rated as the

Once the most important memory is identified, it is usually evident what brought the client into therapy. For instance, assume a client comes in because of increasing depression, and Memory 4 from the EMP—the clearest/most negative early memory identified using the rating scales—describes a situation when the client was abandoned by his mother at age seven. It is a small step to wonder whether there has been a recent loss or breakup of an emotionally significant relationship, when and how that came about, and whether the depression might be linked to that loss. This contrived example is straightforward; in practice, many are not as obvious. The sooner it is determined what brings the client to therapy, the faster one can help clients get their lives back on track.[3] In a particular case, the problem might involve deficits in communication skills; deficiencies in building an emotionally intimate relationship; the unavoidable loss of a relationship that has left the client in a profound grief state; and so forth. The EMP often tells us exactly what is missing; if it doesn't, it will usually point us to what the problem is (here, feelings tied to abandonment) and something about what is causing the client to be stuck (no strategy to avoid abandonment), which can focus the therapy process.

Several colleagues have remarked to me that less well-articulated versions of memories work appear in many strategic therapies, such as Milton Erickson's,[4] which are also designed to identify and provide what is needed to get a client's life back on track (my construction). Strategic therapies require a therapist to be active beyond being an excellent listener; some therapists will not feel comfortable in this role. Haley (1973/1986) pointed out that "therapy can be called strategic if the clinician initiates what happens during therapy and designs a particular approach for each problem" (p. 17). Haley's book (1973/1986) on selected Erickson cases provides examples of how Erickson designed interventions to help clients resolve problems in their lives. Memories work can be conceptualized as often similar to what Erickson did but without intentional hypnosis—my work involves reconfiguring memories as if they embodied a mental template or blueprint that depicts how the mind processes experience. When the revised template becomes operational, the client changes.

Notes

1 The reader looking for a collection of classic early memory articles is encouraged to review Olson's (1979) book, the first edited book on early memories, which collected outstanding papers on early memories written up to the mid 1970s. Ruth Munroe notes in the frontispiece of Olson's book: "Adler's routine request for a first memory was actually the first memory approach toward the projective-test method now so widely used. His first memory technique was . . . unique as a quasi-test device . . . and may be used systematically to reveal deep personality trends." Although Olson's approach is primarily Adlerian, the papers are not exclusively so.
2 Previously, it was assumed by Adlerians that the first recollection was the most important, as they believed it revealed "the style of life." Although I observed what many Adlerians reported, I asked my EMP subjects which memory was most important in their protocol (p. 11). In my sample the sixth memory (clearest or most important of a lifetime) was about as important as the first. If the goal is to find out what memory is most important, it makes sense to ask.
3 Not all therapies are organized to help clients "get their lives back on track," which is commonly the goal of CP therapy. For example, analysis is designed to help clients understand themselves; behaviorists modify behavior; Adlerians address the lifestyle; etc. I view my work as closest to Milton Erickson's (see Schiffman (1998) for a concise summary of Erickson's work) strategic therapy, which also focuses on helping clients become unstuck, but relies primarily on hypnosis as a technique, not memories work.
4 Schiffman (1998) described *strategic therapy* as a type of therapy in which "the therapist is extremely active and directive, dealing with problems head on" (p. 191). Memories work is similarly active. Schiffman summarized a particularly clever Milton Erickson case to illustrate his style of therapy. The patient, who was known only in the psychiatric hospital as George, spoke in a word salad, which he mumbled to himself. In George's sixth year of hospitalization, Erickson became involved. He made a connection with George by inventing his own word salad, which he spoke to George, who countered with voluminous servings of his own. Over time, this pattern was frequently acted out between the two men. Eventually, George gave up, began to speak normally to Erickson, was released by the hospital and, for the next three years, adjusted well until contact was lost. For the record, I view myself as a strategic therapist but do not take cases like George's. I primarily do memories work. Erickson was a master who, with any given case, did whatever was needed to be done, such as invent word salads.

2 Analyzing Early Memories Is Like Learning a New Language and a New Operating System

attempted to write short stories, with just enough skill to appreciate the genius of writers who were truly masters of the craft. Fiction writers and playwrights often seemed to understand memories in ways that psychologists in 1972 did not. They commonly used an individual's important memories in fiction to synthesize and express character and issues deftly and succinctly. Memories also seemed to be intuitively understood by readers of serious literature without a lot of "by the numbers" psychological interpretation. Or so it seemed.

As I imported my literary understanding of memories to psychology, I began to question more closely what I thought I knew from a character's, or a client's, memories. I came to regard memories as a foreign language with its own rules and syntax. Once I had interpreted a thousand or so memories several years into my graduate studies, I found myself having "a-ha!" or "eureka" experiences when I "got" what the memory had to say without a lot of analysis; I just "knew" what the memory said about the character or client. It was, as we used to say in graduate school, "intuitively obvious." As graduate students, we said that about many things we could not explain.

As I challenged my understanding of memories, however, I saw that memories were both history and metaphor. History, obviously, is powerful. It can grab us, hold us in its spell, bend us and mold us, and in extreme cases, change us forever. Often, we are defined by our history. But, as metaphor, memories became lighter, more poetic and ephemeral. As metaphor, they are not simply history; they are not "self-explanatory." They are imbedded thought forms, "as if" ways of thinking and perceiving that capture classes of experiences and preserve them for use in other contexts. They became not just a piece of personal history but forms that were created by that history that have assumed a separate and independent existence. In turn, these memories as metaphors shape current experience so it conforms to perceptions integral to these memories. Memories simultaneously reflect past experience and the forms that mold and shape that past experience until a memory becomes not just itself but a layered archive of experiences that shape shift between history and a metaphorical depiction of history.

For me, that epiphany became a stunning revelation. After, I could no longer view memories the same way. I could now see the memory as a historic event, but also as a container that framed the historic event while it simultaneously revealed the metaphorical mechanism that filtered what was viewed and processed by the observer in present time. Amazing!

Once I understood that memories were both history and metaphor, I intuitively jumped to how they needed to be used in therapy. Clearly, we could not change history, any more than we could get our metaphorical horses back in the barn after the door was left open. What happened, happened. But we could change *something*, and that was how the past was interpreted and constructed. The only thing set in stone was the happening of the event itself, not how we understood it, and certainly not what we chose to make of it as we brought that understanding to our current interactions with the world.

When I grasped this concept, after studying literally thousands of memories and working with dozens of clients, I was transformed. I could no longer view people in the same way. Once I had a set of memories, I could step back into the past, not as a historian exactly, but as someone who could experience the psychological mechanism that shaped and massaged facts and events until a worldview congealed that enabled its owner to function as a coherent human being. As I later became interested in military history, I realized that parties who had been to war with one another would never agree on "who did what to whom"—not because they were pathological liars, but because they used a "mechanism," for lack of a better word, or conceptual device that formed and shaped their opinions about why their group did certain things and why opposing groups acted as they did in response. I was stunned. I would never be able to view countries and political science the same way again.

Now comes the critical question: How can we describe that "mechanism"? What is it, and how does it operate?

I also understood that my immediate goal as a therapist was not to try to recover what was hidden and repressed. I could see that there was often an immense amount of work to do with what was given to me (and obvious to clients as well) once I put their context in words. Just as clients might be held hostage by their own history, they were most certainly held hostage by their construction of that history, which became,

26 *Analyzing Early Memories*

in effect, a trap for similarly resonating experiences that "felt the same way." My goal, as I engaged the memories, was to re-work them with clients so that alternative views of that history were possible. Those perspectives, hopefully, might offer a better and more useful fit between what actually happened and what clients believed happened. I came to

required a mind-set of openness and vulnerability. Worse, it required that they acknowledge they might be wrong about how they saw things in the past and to reject those erroneous beliefs. How easy is it for us to acknowledge on a trip that we have driven 200 miles in the wrong direction and need to turn back? How many fights have begun, before GPS, over whether a turn should have been made at the last junction? These are trivial matters in relation to having gone years awry on one's life journey! What humility and courage are required to abandon our mistakes and begin anew with a philosophical shrug of our shoulders!

How do I work with a set of EMP memories? I put them on and try to see with them as if I had slipped on my clients' personal reality glasses. I want to see what my clients see, think how they think, and react as they do while experiencing their lives and important relationships. Memories provide a template that depicts a memory language system and the individual's apperceptual process. How exactly to do this will be detailed in Chapter 5. Once I see, feel, and understand what is not working in clients' lives after experiencing their memories, I begin to suggest alternative paths: "Yes I understand how you view the present interaction, after experiencing X with your mother, but I am wondering if there might be another explanation for what happened then and what is happening now. Let's think about this together again."

3 A Diagnostic System That Focuses on Where a Client Is Stuck Helps Us Craft More Precise Interventions

Autobiographical memory theory helps us understand what needs to be prioritized in insight-oriented therapy. To do that, we need to ask two critical questions: "What makes us recall what we do?" and "what makes us recall what we do in the way that we do?" Without answers to these questions, we often fail to understand what makes a client become stuck, and, as a result, as therapists we become stuck, too.

Let me offer an example of a client I briefly treated for post-traumatic stress disorder (PTSD). Despite the lack of a specific "trauma," she had been put on Social Security Disability the preceding four years. She needed a reevaluation to continue on disability. What proximally caused the presumed trauma five years before was an episodic situation in her workplace. The client believed that she was well qualified for positions involving a promotion that she had interviewed for over a several-year period, but she was always rejected. She filed a complaint with the Equal Employment Opportunity Commission (EEOC), which took more than a year to be adjudicated. Her complaint was eventually upheld, and her employer (ironically, the federal government) was soundly reprimanded. But the process was so debilitating for her that she developed symptoms of PTSD, including severe depression and anxiety, agitation, and a sleep disorder. She was placed on disability and seen by a psychiatrist in individual therapy for approximately three years. When I saw her for a reevaluation, following his retirement, I started with an EMP, which was used to better understand her presenting problem. The EMP requires about three hours of introspection and writing outside the office, and many clients report when they bring their protocols in for an interpretative session that they now understand their troubles in a way that had previously eluded them. Often, the presumed causative experience never appears in the EMP.

My client's PTSD-related memory dated to an incident when she was a teenager in her large family. A thrifty, planful person, she had been saving change in a glass jar; she wanted to use the money for a "rainy day." Her older sister and an older brother stole her money and delighted in telling her how they spent it. She asserted herself and made the problem

28   A Diagnostic System

known to her father, who said and did nothing. Her stepmother was appropriately sympathetic and upset at her siblings' behavior and spoke to her husband. Bottom line: Nothing happened.

How was the theft when she was a teen related to the PTSD that developed when she did not obtain a promotion? My client learned from

the perpetrators to gloat and humiliate her—certainly there could be no conceivable rationale for that in any fair and just world! In expressing my profound outrage at this injustice, I validated her own feelings, which had not been validated by her father. As I ranted on, she began to feel better almost immediately. Moreover, I suggested that she talk with her stepmother and her father and then with her brother. In so many words, I suggested a redo of the injustice perpetrated with her family. Fortunately, all parties did much better than their initial performance years previous. She subsequently reported a further reduction in her usual stress level. Within three sessions she felt ready to return to work—just not at the same agency where she had been victimized. As it is said, truly, once burned, twice learned.

Could this client have been treated with medications or insight-oriented therapy or with eye movement desensitization and reprocessing (EMDR; Shapiro, 1989)? She was in fact treated by her psychiatrist with medications and supportive therapy, and from her description she gained from the process—just not what was needed to return to work. Sometimes the simplest and most direct approach needs to be tried first. I undertook the EMP evaluation to determine who she was before her work environment damaged her. Once she understood the historic antecedents and how her recent traumatic experiences were profoundly wrong on several levels, to some extent she was able to let go of her bad feelings. Her hurt and anger had been expressed and heard. I gave her as true and real a reaction to the theft of her funds as I could and lamented the lack of an appropriate response from her parents. She was ready to move on. She could accept her family as it was with its flaws and imperfections. They did much better the second time around. Their response now was "good enough."

Early in my career I used to talk about "unfinished business" that is captured in memories—especially in very clear, extremely negative memories. It is difficult to find a more apt example of unfinished business than this memory and this case. The work of therapy here? To complete what was unfinished, particularly to validate her feelings, especially regarding unfairness.

What about using EMDR? The preceding clinical example illustrates my biggest reservation with Parnell's (2007) otherwise skillful practice of EMDR: What is it we treat when someone with a traumatic history presents for help? Are we treating a trauma, or are we treating a construction of minimally related events that continue to cause psychological harm, much like a recently acquired pebble in a shoe revivifies an earlier foot injury?

EMDR recognizes that the past is alive in the present. Bruhn (2008) noted that Parnell (2007) talked about the importance of "memory networks" (p. 10), but she provided few examples of techniques to access and deconstruct these networks. And therein lies the rub. Rather than work through the feelings using clinical material, Shapiro, her mentor, apparently asked clients to rapidly move their eyes back and forth, which presumably releases the tension (anxiety) bound up in the memory. Is this method efficacious? This is what Shapiro (1999) said: "EMDR appears to be effective in reducing at least some indices of distress relative to no-treatment in a number of anxiety conditions, including posttraumatic stress disorder, panic disorder, and public-speaking anxiety. Second, EMDR appears at least as effective or more effective than several non-validated treatments (e.g., relaxation, active listening) for posttraumatic stress reactions" (p. 5). Shapiro claimed it is efficacious, but her method lacks face validity, a requirement that psychological treatment methods commonly satisfy. It seems, for example, that one could just as easily ask clients to count backward from 100 by 3s or stand up on one foot and twirl counterclockwise as ask them to move their eyes back and forth rapidly. To put it plainly, the secret of Shapiro's method may be that she tasks clients to do "something" while they stay engaged with the memory and its feelings. The empirical question, in my opinion, is whether the "something" that Shapiro asks her clients to do is as remedial and as healing as inviting them, per the present case, to confront their fears and work through the feelings. That appears to be a sensible research question to test.

Bruhn and Last (1982) described four theories of early memories—Adlerian, ego-psychological, Freudian, and Cognitive-Perceptual (CP; see Table 0.1). Later, Bruhn (1990a, b) expanded CP theory. Practitioners of EMDR need to revisit autobiographical memory to consider how the past lives in the present and what can be done to detoxify schematic experiences

30 A Diagnostic System

that cause mischief. So, too, with other insight-oriented methods. In my judgment, it is here that we struggle most as clinicians: What can we do to help clients understand and resolve problems that have left them stuck in their own process and frustrated with their lives? I'm not convinced that asking clients to follow a pencil back and forth while they focus on

4 When We Don't Understand a Client's Needs, We Can Cause Damage

Years ago, I worked in a psychiatric practice with a brilliant psychiatrist. I would send my own children to him if they needed help.

My colleague was about to go on an extended summer vacation, well deserved, the first he had taken of this length since he began his practice years before. He was professional and appropriate in his approach. Well in advance he announced his plan to his patients. One, however, became increasingly disturbed as his vacation date drew near. Worried, he asked me to work with her until he returned. I agreed. As his vacation became imminent, he remarked that she was becoming so agitated that he feared a psychotic break. His concern was justified. He gave me detailed instructions as to hospitalization, should her situation worsen. I took careful notes. Her emotional state was in fact dire.

When I saw the patient, I began to collect her autobiographical memories in session, not in her own hand as I would several years later after publishing the EMP. One of her first memories was as follows:

> I remember my parents leaving on vacation. We had a circular drive in front of our home [a huge estate]. I finally realized they would be going without me. I burst into tears and ran out the front door after them as their limousine began to pull away. As I ran into the drive and shouted for them to stop, crying uncontrollably, our guard dogs broke away, growling fearsomely, barking loudly, and jumped on me, knocking me down. I was terrified. They must not have heard me. They kept driving away.

Obviously, the patient had a latent separation/abandonment issue that was triggered on cue by her therapist's leaving her while he went with his wife and family on vacation—a much gentler version of how she recalled her parents had abandoned her.

In those days there was no fully articulated cognitive-perceptual theory (Bruhn, 1990a) and no EMP. Had it been available, my colleague could have known his patient's vulnerability before he left on vacation. And so it is in many clinical crises—we do not know, and when we innocently open

32 *Understanding a Client's Needs*

Fibber McGee's psychic closet, whatever is stashed away for future work comes crashing down upon us.

As I worked with the patient, I pointed out that she was primed to expect abandonment, that she expected not to be heard, and that she expected any cries of protest on her part to be met with violent disap-

working relationship with him. She was fine when he came back. They talked productively about what happened, and both understood where her feelings were coming from. Being able to do brief memories work saved (at that time) at least a 21-day hospitalization for a psychotic episode, anti-psychotic medications, and a new trauma conflated with her girlhood trauma of being abandoned.

Part of the Hippocratic oath is "First, do no harm." Or, more precisely, "I will prescribe regimens for the good of my patients according to my ability and my judgment and never do harm to anyone." My colleague did that. He foresaw the potential danger and asked me to stand in for him. The EMP now helps reduce risk to patients, which must be our first concern as medical professionals. Once we understand what the vulnerability is, we have a much better understanding of how to avoid it or plan around it.

A Common Clinician Error Before Beginning Therapy

At the beginning of therapy most clinicians commonly ask some variant of the question, "What brings you in?" The client replies with something like, "I'm going through a divorce" or "I'm having issues with my parents over how I'm raising my son" or "my partner has been getting increasingly abusive with me."

If the therapist responds with some variant of, "That sounds awful. Let's talk about when this began," the assessment part of the initial interview is soon likely to became history. What do I mean by that? If you respond to something like this, you will be focusing on the tip of the iceberg, not what lies beneath.

Perhaps an example will help. In the process of completing their EMPs, as many as 30% of new clients will report memories they have never told anyone else, including previous therapists and counselors (evident in EMP, p. 30). The following is an example.

A colleague referred a patient (Bruhn, 1995a) because he was working with the wife (see Chapter 1). He concluded that the marriage was broken and not repairable. The husband, whom he was referring to me, was seeing a younger woman. The wife, my colleague believed, was sexually frigid and not interested in sex whereas the girlfriend and the husband were sexually compatible. The plan was to continue to see the couple separately and to work on any additional issues that might arise from the separation and probable divorce. My colleague's assessment was sound and made sense clinically as I began to work with the husband. I came to the same conclusion until I read the EMP I later asked him to fill out.

I saw the husband for a couple of sessions, sensed that something was not adding up, and prevailed upon him to complete an EMP, which he did. The following was his second memory (the protocol is available in edited format in Bruhn, 1995a).

EM 2: Our scoutmaster used to invite us to work on merit badges at his home on Sunday and would molest me while his wife was at church singing in the choir.

Change: Try to understand why I didn't immediately go to my parents and tell . . .

Your interpretation of a memory: I think my early traumatic experience with control of the scoutmaster was one of the major causes of my lack of sensitivity toward people and especially women. The early sexual feelings were good but in the male environment being forced upon me caused embarrassment and my sense of why am I being picked on like this . . . Took a long time to realize women feel and can be friends rather than sexual objects.

(Bruhn, 1995a, pp. 292–295)

Initially, my colleague and I viewed the case as follows: Man marries woman who is frigid sexually, finds a lover whom he is more compatible with, then requests a divorce. After the EMP we saw things differently: A man is sexually abused as an 11-year-old, doubts his masculinity, does not tell his parents, and goes on to marry a woman who is uninterested in sex. In so many words, my client then became a "sexual predator" and assumed the role of the scoutmaster who abused him. He immediately saw what was happening when I discussed this with him. But what to do now?

34 Understanding a Client's Needs

I suggested he talk to his parents and call the police—a Child Protection Services contact. His parents were shocked but glad that he told them after all these years. The police told him that he would not be needed to testify, as dozens of other victims had already volunteered, and the scoutmaster's trial was imminent. The trial was sensational, as one might

The EMP alerted all parties to what was going on under the surface of what seemed like a heated but not terribly unusual midlife affair. The couple divorced relatively quickly and painlessly after it was clear to both what had precipitated the affair. The husband saw that he needed to work on owning his own needs while being more real and transparent with others. His conversations with his parents were very helpful in discussing real experiences with people who loved and cared about him. Once he experienced being transparent with his parents, and not alienating them, it was much easier to be open with his girlfriend.

The original case of what looked like mismatched libidos took a decidedly different course after the husband's history of abuse as a Boy Scout became the initial focus in his treatment.

Cases involving undisclosed sexual abuse are much more common than many clinicians believe. The EMP is likely to yield a shockingly high number of such cases—roughly 30% of clients reported previously undisclosed memories even after 10 years or more of therapy. To cite something recently in the news, in 2018 Catholics in America are reporting thousands of cases of sexual abuse to Pennsylvania authorities now finally willing to listen to them and take action.

Another example of this pattern follows.

I once was contacted by a journalist who told me she wanted to do a story on memories work, which she did. I suggested she complete an EMP so she would have a more personal perspective. She did.

Her second EM was being sexually molested by her second-grade teacher. She had not reported the abuse to her parents or to anyone, not even her analyst of ten years. I innocently asked two respected analytic colleagues about how an analysis could continue for ten years with no work at all on this very serious incident of sexual abuse. Both shrugged and said in so many words, "It is the patient's responsibility to bring up such matters in analysis." I responded, "If you were a physician practicing physical medicine, would you have the same attitude about physical diseases in a new patient?" For instance, assume a patient was previously treated for breast cancer. Would you have any responsibility for making an inquiry about past medical problems?

I think most of us would agree that physicians have a responsibility to make such an inquiry. My experience is that most physicians require a written medical history from their new patients. But many mental health practitioners do not believe they have a parallel responsibility to inquire about patient traumas. The EMP can help with what I believe should be a routine part of our professional responsibility. I also know that many of my fellow professionals will not agree. This area of how we function as professionals might benefit from public debate. One consequence of failing to inquire in the past? The many thousands of cases of sexual abuse that we do not know about until decades later.

What happened with the journalist? I suggested she tell her parents and her analyst. She did. I am not sure how these disclosures affected her afterward. But she said she was relieved. During her adult years she told me she had never had a serious romantic relationship. I believe those two events are not unrelated. The material she wrote about memories work that she showed me was on point.

Odd to report, perhaps, but I sometimes wondered about the wife of the man molested by the scoutmaster and whether she, like the journalist, had also been molested. This connection is completely speculative, certainly, but it is common knowledge that those who have been sexually molested are often conflicted about their sexuality.

What is clear, to me at least, is that the more pertinent background we know about the people we work with, especially their sexual histories, the more likely we are to be able to help them.

5 Bergson's Dilemma, or How Utility Actually Operates

the memories to my class, and free-associated to them—for example, "This is an individual who is triggered by abandonment experiences, and then reacts full throttle when he believes he has been left." Then a life-changing event occurred. One brave student approached me after class in my office as I basked in the afterglow of a performance well done and said, "I can understand some of what you said about the memories, but I understood only after you interpreted the memories. I thought your insights were amazing!"

The student merited a post-doctoral degree in diplomacy.

I was dumbstruck. I believed everyone understood the significance of these memories. I thought their meaning was intuitively obvious. After all, early memories contained *perceptographs*[1] that one could extract from the memory to see the world as the client did. But thanks to my courageous student, I now knew otherwise. I had not been seeking a compliment. But I now had a problem. How to explain what I thought "everyone" knew?

I spent a good deal of summer break, protocols stacked on my desk, beginning with an intuitive understanding of my clients' memories while pressing myself to explain, more clearly than I ever attempted before, how I knew what I thought I did. I found this experience vexing to the extreme. How could I teach what I thought I knew when a rational explanation eluded *me*?

For days I worried these memories for answers. Then I had an epiphany. I was aware I was keying on the client's expectations in problematic situations. But I had to find a way to operationalize what I was doing or

How Utility Actually Operates 37

continue to experience a less than optimal result teaching it. How did I know what I thought I knew about these memories? What an aggravation! As I ruminated and, resigned to apparent failure, began to let go of my frustration, the following formula emerged (literally), as if written on a white storyboard, from the mists of my unconscious: "When x occurs, I expect y to follow."

Stunned, I wrote this formula down on the back of an envelope on my desk before it faded to oblivion. As I eagerly applied this formula to dozens of memories, racing frenetically from one to the next, I quickly discovered something that I did not expect.

I observed this formula worked perfectly with some memories but not at all for others. Why the inconsistency? Now more aggravation!

After testing several hundred memories, I began to see that the formula worked in nearly every case for memories that were predominantly negative in affective tone. For positive affect memories, the formula rarely worked. "What the hell is going wrong?" I groused to myself, greatly annoyed.

I looked at memories with predominantly positive affect, of the sort, "We always went to Grandma's for Sunday dinner after church." I pulled a sample.[2] I intuited these memories appeared to be serving a different function than did negative affect memories. Then it came to me. The positive memories appeared to express strong needs or something close to what Freud might have called wishes, such as "I like (enjoy) spending time with family under pleasant (nurturing) circumstances." I realized that I had been ignoring these during class demonstrations in favor of negative affect memories. Why? They did not tell me much about the client's issue, or so it seemed—less, certainly, than negative affect memories. When the positive memories referred to recurring events (Sunday dinners at Grandma's), the probability that they reflected needs appeared to be even stronger and more certain. But what about Freud's wishes? That was simple. "Needs gratified" can function as "wishes fulfilled," as in, "I wish we went to Grandma's more often because good things happen." A-ha! I had put a couple of pieces together!

On the other hand, recurring memories with a strong negative texture appeared to depict strong fears. For instance: "Dad used to go out drinking Friday nights after work, and when he came home he used to pull us out of bed and give us a whipping." ("Why?") "Because he was angry." The recurring nature of the experience suggested a deeply ingrained set of negative expectations. Here, the expectations might be expressed as, "When people become frustrated or angry, I expect they will take their feelings out on me." When the situation referred to is repetitive and very negative, I surmised, we must rule out PTSD or a similar disorder that culminates in a loss of trust, paranoia, strong anxiety, and the like. Clients who have memories similar in form, I noticed from my knowledge of the sample, often required long-term therapy because they had not learned to distinguish who is "safe" from who is "dangerous" (like Dad when

38 *How Utility Actually Operates*

drunk), and that differentiation required time and repetitions. Trust, and with it a sense of security, is difficult to rebuild after being lost.

In the later 1980s as I looked at the happiest memory in Part II of the EMP, I had another epiphany: The most negative/clearest memory in Part I and the happiest memory in Part II commonly fit together like a hand

might depict closeness and connection.

I realized these intensely negative expectations permeated issues that had never been adequately processed and resolved. I could finally describe what had actually brought the client into treatment, even though the ostensible presenting problem (e.g., depression, grief, trouble holding a job, problems with the opposite sex) might appear very different. It was at this nexus of strong feelings and negative expectations that therapy had to be directed for clients to become unstuck and move on with their lives.

This insight profoundly shaped my understanding of what memories work did and where it needed to be directed.

I owe much to my student who confessed that she did not understand how I interpreted memories. This critical experience pushed me to engage the limits of my own understanding and to back-engineer how memory operates and express that process formulaically, so anyone could do what I did. In the process I discovered how differences between positive and negative affect memories lead them to perform complementary functions. Once I deduced that each handles a different function, I could decipher the role of each (and their interplay) in autobiographical memory. Positive affect memories orient us to what we need, and negative affect memories help to clarify where we are stuck in our lives (what we need to resolve), given our expectations. As I continued in this vein, I realized how Bergson's thoughts on the utility of memory (we recall what is useful) needed elaboration—for instance, positive affect memories function differently than negative ones, even though both follow the principle of utility. It may sound odd to say it this way, but I had begun

How Utility Actually Operates 39

to decode a "Rosetta stone" of memories written in perceptographic language to lawful rules in English.

As this process of exploration continued, I realized that some of these memories I had collected focused on *contexts* that appeared to be troublesome for the person who recalled them. This context was dramatically captured and preserved by the memory. I next proposed the *précis method* of memory interpretation for negative affect memories:[4]

Précis: When *x* occurs, I expect *y* to follow.

To illustrate what happens when we reverse-engineer a negative affect memory, let's summarize the patient's separation memory in Chapter 4:

"When I am about to be abandoned and express my apprehensions and anxieties, I expect not to be heard." As expressed by the formula, **When *x* occurs, I expect *y* to follow.** In both cases—her parents leaving for vacation and her therapist leaving for vacation—her concerns are not heard. She felt extremely vulnerable. Even when expressed, her feelings had no impact. In the first case, she cried out for her parents and was not heard; in the second, she became agitated to the point of becoming psychotic and believed, once again, she had not been heard and her feelings were not important to her therapist. The close similarity in form suggests that the expectations evident in the memory are resonating with her current expectations. Once the pattern was evident to her and the solution proposed, her intensely disorganizing feelings diminished almost immediately (she felt heard), providing additional evidence that the hypothesis was correct and the cause of her being stuck had been addressed and remedied.[5] Did I "cure" her in one session with this intervention? No. I worked through a critical incident in her memory, reinterpreted it, provided her with an opportunity to practice speaking up and being heard, and returned her to her therapist to continue what I conceptualized as skill building (speaking up effectively) and thereby rebuilding trust.

In workshops I am sometimes asked why I think the précis method is important. My answer? Without the précis, we free associate to the memory, and inter-judge reliability suffers. Professionally, we would be left with "some people can work effectively with memories; some people can't." Without a high level of reliability, the validity of interpretations is suspect. And worse: We would have no method to teach memory interpretation, only a variety of opinions about what a memory might mean and what caused the client to seek therapy. My student's feedback caused me to look at memories afresh and to discover, through a process of back-engineering, that negative contextual expectations are imbedded in the core of a negative affect memory.

Without the précis to do memory interpretation, we have art, but we do not have science.[6]

The précis is used with negative affect memories. But what happens when we collect a group of memories, aggregated in Part I of the EMP by

40 *How Utility Actually Operates*

requests to recall memories linked by association ("What memory comes to mind . . .")? If pleasant memories are requested, the subject will produce them; if negative, the subject will produce those. But not inevitably. If I ask for the earliest memory and then a memory that comes to mind by association, I am asking for the memory that comes to mind next tied to

protocols. The clearest/most negative memory best depicts perceptographically the unresolved issue that is interfering with the client's life progress. Stated simply, the principle of utility operates in the EMP to spotlight the memory (clearest)[7] that best reveals the major unresolved issue (clearest/most negative memory). The remaining memories in Part I commonly add detail as the problem is elaborated. The principle of attraction—subordinate to Bergson's principle of utility—helps to identify the memory that is most significant and what underlying issue needs to be resolved while other memories depict aspects of the problem in the clearest/most negative memory.

In hindsight, negative expectations, seen in the interplay of associated needs and fears, reveal how Bergson's principle of utility is played out in the choice and shaping of autobiographical memories. We now not only understand how personal memory is organized from Bergson (by utility), we also know how best to understand the memories we obtain from the EMP—via the précis, and through how needs (positive affect memories) and fears (negative affect memories) play off each other. We now not only know what causes clients to become stuck, we also understand, by reverse-engineering memories, how the principle of utility operates to organize the content, form, and affect of autobiographical memories. These memories also provide clues as to how we can help clients get unstuck and move forward with their lives.

As my work with memories became known in the early 1980s, I received mail from Soviet academics requesting information on how I worked. Uneasy, I called the CIA and made them aware of Soviet

How Utility Actually Operates 41

interest and requested their counsel. Three agents met with me at The George Washington University. They examined the mail in detail and photographed it. I knew how powerful this technique was, and its implications, but I wondered if they did. After the consultation and a delay of several weeks, I was told to carry on: no restrictions on my publishing. I still did not feel comfortable, nor did several colleagues who warned me about the potential misuse of this method,[8] so I delayed publication of a major paper.

The paper in question involved collecting memories from a key historic figure via books, public statements, interviews and the like toward the end of approximating Part I of the EMP. I eventually simplified the process and selected Ben Franklin as my subject of choice, partly due to his familiarity to scholars and his long and well-documented public life. I might add that it is probably not an accident that Franklin appears on the $100 bill, as he was not only an important patriot, he was the Bill Gates of his generation—fabulously wealthy and prominent through his printing business. I identified Franklin's specific memories through his leaving Boston, where he had apprenticed in the printing trade, to breaking his apprenticeship, running away to Philadelphia, and beginning life independently. What was especially noteworthy to me in this analysis of Franklin's simulated Part I EMP (Bruhn, 2006) is Franklin reported that he was physically abused by his brother—likely his clearest/most negative memory. As a result, I suggested in the paper that Franklin may have been the firebrand who sustained the colony's rebellion from England. His motivation? Franklin was no longer willing to continue to suffer abuse from a harsh, powerful master. In the first instance with his brother, he modeled independence; in the second he strongly advocated for it. When England began to abuse America, Franklin may have taken it personally and willed it to end.

There is much that can be learned about an individual's psychological makeup from simulated Part I EMPs. I am hesitant to discuss it too specifically in a public forum like this one.

Notes

1 In a memory, a *perceptograph* consolidates how the individual sees the world— what emerges as a figure to ground in psychological space. In recollections perceptographs consolidate the essential psychological structure of the memory, the bones and sinews of what makes it work as a remembered experience. A perceptograph draws from our needs, our interests, and important issues that are currently in process, and it depicts this material as a visual product that reveals the essential structure of the memory. For instance, a sad memory of a pet dying may convey as a perceptograph: "I become greatly upset when I experience the loss of an attachment figure."

2 By the late 1980s, when I was working on preliminary versions of the EMP, I made a small advancement. I observed that some memories were both positive and negative in tone, with emotional highs and lows. I surmised that a memory

42 *How Utility Actually Operates*

was positive for a client if it ended positively, but in specific instances I would not have bet much. I decided to ask clients to rate their own memories for affective tone (see EMP, pp. 9–10), which reduced the scope of the problem. But a small minority could not rate the affective tone of their memories—their feelings were blocked. They literally did not know how certain things felt. This is not an issue that the clinician can explore with clients directly: "Can

viewed as a mechanistic metatheory by Pepper, which tells us the two systems, cognitive-perceptual and psychoanalytic, are independent and incompatible philosophically with one another. Put another way, each model offers an independent explanation of how the mind operates. Each model explains what happens in terms unique to its own metatheory. Psychoanalytic theory, which is organized to explain the flow and movement of psychic energy, focuses on the process of repression—that is, what causes certain material to be repressed and how that material can be brought to consciousness. Cognitive-perceptual theory is not designed to explain mechanistic processes, and psychoanalytic theory is not designed to explain contextual phenomena. They are independent metatheories designed to explain different phenomena.

5 I have occasionally been asked, "Do you think EMDR could produce equally effective results? You help clients resolve issues evident in negative memories, but the two methods may be equally effective." My answer? This is an empirical question. Create equivalent groups and run the two conditions. Essentially, we would be testing finger- or pencil-waving (EMDR) against memory interpretation and skills building (memories work) against something like listening to relaxing music as a control condition.

6 What evidence is there that mental health professionals can master the précis method? In the 1980s and 1990s, I offered workshops to mental health professionals and taught the précis method, using single memories and asking for volunteers to derive the précis from the memory. Using this method, I taught several thousand professionals how to derive a précis. During that time, I cannot recall a single person who left a six-hour workshop not being able to précis a memory, but let's say 5% struggled to master the method. Granted, some memories are complex, but when we look for the clearest part, that step will take us to where the memory itself is focused. For those who want to self-teach, I have included EMP protocols in the following, and each contains multiple précis: Bruhn (1990a, 1992a, b, 1995a, 2006) and Richards (1993, Appendix C).

How Utility Actually Operates 43

7 The clearest memory is such because it pulls a disproportional amount of psychic energy. The clearest memory that also has the most intensely negative affect points us to the context that is most problematic for the client *now*. The clearest memory with the most intensely positive affect highlights the strongest needs, which are in deficit presently because of the problematic aspects depicted in the memory with the most negative affect.

8 On July 6, 2017, I was listening to a piece on President Trump's first visit to a G20 gathering in Poland. He was to meet with Vladimir Putin one on one during the visit. The commentator pointed out Putin was a "master manipulator" and cited as an example how he learned that German Chancellor Angela Merkel was afraid of dogs from one of her early memories. Putin brought his pet Labrador to his meeting with her. Once we know an individual's triggers, we can manipulate them to their detriment or focus on helping them via memories work to resolve these issues. I hope the antecedents of my work did not fall into the hands of a young Mr. Putin in 1982. Like many things, regretfully, memories work can be used for good or ill.

6 Memories Are Programmed by the Mind

pens, we employ follow-up questions to unbundle what the memory might mean—sometimes a tedious process. The point? No single method, no matter how powerful, will work with everyone.

Question: Once we have the story, how can we reverse-engineer the process that created it?

The mind, operating in its constructive, programming role, uses several common tools, most of which we identified in the previous section. These are specified below.

1 The story, with a beginning, middle and end, has a point to make. How can we determine what the point is? The point can usually be inferred by how the story ends. For example, let's say that the memory concerns struggling to develop a skill and persisting through many failures until success occurs. The point? Set a goal, persist, and success will come. What drives the selection of such experiences? A need to master and achieve and a strategy for how to increase the probability of success. If especially significant, this need will often be found in other memories linked by association.

2 The story can usually be described by one of the 15 embedded content or process themes (CEMSS-R, Section VII; Last & Bruhn, 1991), which have demonstrated an acceptable level of inter-judge reliability (Richards, Bruhn, Lucente, & Casey, 2015). These themes commonly involve the following: (a) bonding with a primary object, (b) security, (c) trust, and (d) mastery. These higher order developmental objectives are evident as we scan the themes for higher order needs.

Memories Are Programmed by the Mind   45

3 Psychic energy, which manifests in the memory by the degree of clarity. Very clear memories are the functional equivalent of a larger font size, bold face, and italic type in printing. All speak to the importance of what is being reported. The mind programs messages about importance via clarity.
4 Affective quality. Positive affect points to wishes and needs. Negative affect to unresolved issues and traumas.
5 Very clear memories with very positive affect suggest high priority needs, which are likely in deficit now, in proportion to the degree of clarity.
6 Very clear memories with very negative affect point to contexts that trigger the individual because the issues referenced in the memory have not been adequately resolved and therefore remain in process. Very clear, strongly negative affect memories depict *key traumas* that must be dealt with before the individual can comfortably move on to other matters. The context and the associated expectations are strongly responsive to recurring triggers.
7 Very clear memories with very negative affect spotlight the problem that brings the client in for treatment. Very clear memories with very positive affect depict possible avenues to bring the problem to resolution. To offer a simple example: A memory where a client was beaten and rejected sketches out the form of the problem—an expectation of poor treatment from others. A very clear, positive memory of being praised for an achievement suggests how to resolve it—to please others by meeting goals. In the assessment process, the examiner is looking for forms that describe problem–solution. Ideally, we want to move beyond describing the problem and leaving it up to the therapist to figure out how to resolve it.

Table 6.1 How Memories Are Programmed

Variable	Description/Function
Material organized as a story	Has beginning, middle, and ending. There is a clearest part and strongest feeling. Has a "point"/ message, which can be deduced from the ending.
Intensity/clarity	Range: Very unclear to exceptionally clear. Intensity of spotlighting (signifies importance).
Affective quality	Positive to negative: Wishes (positive, what is needed) to resolve issues (negative, issues in process). What I want more of in my life vs. what makes me unhappy.
Combination 1: Exceptionally clear/ Very positive affect	Spotlights what is needed most in life now.

(continued)

46 Memories Are Programmed by the Mind

Table 6.1 (continued)

Variable	Description/Function
Combination 2: Exceptionally clear/ Very negative affect*	Spotlights most significant unresolved current issue in life and expectations triggered in that context

egies used to program key elements of a memory. Previously, I have described memories as perceptographs, or forms that reflect how the mind is organized, and how memory and personality operate in tandem. Autobiographical memory reflects key elements of the personality; as autobiographical memory is impacted by experience, it in turn causes the personality to adapt as needed, consistent with Darwinian principles of evolution. We make inferences and adapt to survive and thrive as best we can, according to our current understanding.

As issues are resolved in therapy, new issues become ascendant, which are ordinarily reflected in the choice and organization of memories in the EMP. I think of autobiographical memory as a sort of card deck that has been shuffled, with new cards being added and old cards dropped as they become less pertinent. Commonly I have to re-administer the EMP to clients who are changing rapidly in therapy to clarify for both of us where we are as old issues are resolved and replaced.

Of course, not every professional who deals with memories sees things the way I have described. Freud's position is well known, that unbearably negative memories are repressed so the individual can function in life with minimal disruption. Unquestionably Freud is correct: Repression does occur in some cases with respect to certain extremely negative, traumatic memories. Nothing more needs to be said about these. My view comes into play when we nagivate a large universe of memories that can be accessed by the EMP. Freud for the most part was not interested in these kinds of memories because his focus was on how to bring repressed memories to consciousness.

Memories Are Programmed by the Mind 47

Alfred Adler wrote extensively about the earliest memory. He emphasized its importance in what he called *the style of life*. Munroe (1955) acknowledged Adler's pioneering role in the use of the earliest recollection thusly:

> Adler's routine request for a first memory was actually the first approach toward the *projective* test methodology now so widely used. Adler knew very well that the first memory is realistically often incorrect, that its chronology is often suspect. His idea was that the item selected as "first" was *creatively* selected, and could be interpreted in relation to the total personality. Adler's notion of comparing people on the basis of their spontaneous "conscious" reaction to a fairly simple but dynamic question is the very core of contemporary projective techniques.
>
> (Munroe, 1955, pp. 428–429, *n*.)

Although I agree with Adler that the first memory is creatively selected, often inaccurate historically, but projectively significant, I would assert that similar remarks could also be made regarding later memories. For instance, a memory of failing fourth grade, being seriously injured in sixth grade, losing a parent at 12 years of age, being raped at age 15, or having your first child at age 20 may well be as important, or even more important to the development of the personality as the first recollection, and that is exactly what I have found in with clinical subjects who took the EMP. In fact, the "most important memory of a lifetime" (Memory 6) was just as likely to be most important as the first memory as rated by the client. This finding, I might add parenthetically, needs to be tested in a matched sample of clinical and nonclinical subjects. Until then, what I am reporting is clinical observation derived from tabulating responses to approximately 100 EMPs.

I also agree with Adler that the first memory is often important, and perhaps it is more so in Adler's scheme because he uses it to assess the "style of life," which I do not do. In a clinical assessment I am looking for "load-bearing memories," which tend to be the clearest/most negative memory in Part I of the EMP (*spontaneous* memories) but may also relate to a major need that is critical to an individual's psyche.

Adler and I agree on most key points about memories, and I have read his papers and books with great interest, especially early in my career. Here is where we begin to diverge in our view of autobiographical memories, namely in his view that earliest memories are special. Saul, Snyder, and Sheppard (1956) argued:

> Earliest memories are absolutely specific, distinctive, and characteristic for each individual; moreover, they reveal, probably more clearly than any other single psychodynamic datum, the central core of each

48 *Memories Are Programmed by the Mind*

person's psychodynamics, his chief motivations, form of neurosis, and emotional problems.

(p. 229)

I agree that the earliest memories can be used thusly, but I would also

How does Mollon handle trauma? In his foreword to Mollon's book (2002), Fonagy wrote:

> Clinicians still have to work with their patients' past in the present to help them to a better future. We may understand the functioning of memory better from a biological standpoint than we ever have before, yet neurobiology is of little assistance when the clinician is confronted with an individual in a state of despair and confusion, suffering from intrusive thoughts and feelings concerning the past and a dread of the future.

(p. viii)

I appreciate Mollon's book, but terms like *trauma* are virtually useless when we work with clients who have real problems. My suggestion? The clearest most negative spontaneous memory in Part I of the EMP is most likely to depict the issue where the client is ready to begin his own personal work in therapy. What about "an inappropriate sexual experience" in Part II of the EMP? In Chapter 1 I described working with a young woman whose response to that probe described her being sexually molested by her favorite uncle. I immediately jumped to *betrayal* as I read her account of this experience. Puzzled, as this memory was far worse from my perspective than any of her Part I memories, I inquired as to why this memory had not been mentioned earlier in her protocol. She smiled and told me, "I knew you would think this was worse, but

Memories Are Programmed by the Mind   49

it wasn't. My uncle treated me better than anyone else in my family. He treated me as special. I knew you would think it was traumatic, but frankly, I don't."

When she told me this, I immediately recalled the words of my early mentor, Walter Klopfer, for 25 years the editor of the *Journal of Personality Assessment* and a valued friend: "In the world of the blind, the one-eyed man is king." The way it seemed from her protocol was that her uncle was clearly the best of a horrific lot, and I just had not understood how bad her life had been. What would have been terribly traumatic for many barely moved the needle for her.

For my client, her uncle was "king." He was special. Being sexually molested by him was a special and valued treatment. Odd as that sounded to my ears, it rang true to hers.

She did not continue therapy with me after a few sessions. If I could not appreciate her special feelings for her uncle, and if I could not accept him for whom he was, how could I understand her? It took me a while to appreciate what she was telling me. I had been trained professionally to believe that sexual abuse was always wrong, the more so by relatives. It is. But many clients have been so poorly treated by the adults in their lives that, from their perspective, what is unacceptable to us as professionals is recalled as the very best treatment they have ever experienced. Unfortunately, for many of us, "bad" experiences, in the absence of competition, can be experienced as "good" by some clients.

We are always well advised to begin where our clients are, not where we think they should be.

7 The Mind Affects the Body Even as the Body Affects the Mind

her patient for memories work, little understanding how, or if at all, her sarcoidosis might be helped.

What to say to a patient like this? I told her that my colleague had referred her for memories work, and that I was confident that we could make progress on the issues in her memories, but we would have to meet frequently, preferably three sessions a week, given the uncertain amount of time available to us. I asked her for her memories, which she related face to face in session, since the EMP had not yet been published. I transcribed them.

Her first memory was lying on her stomach on the ground as a very young girl looking under her house, which was built on stubby cement blocks. As she peered into the dark, beyond the white wooden lattice, and her eyes adjusted to diminished light, she could see many thick cobwebs, spiders, and other bugs and creepy things. She was frightened at what she saw. Terrified!

What to do with a memory like this? I assumed, for clinical purposes, that whatever the memory was about, her sarcoidosis was probably implicated in some way. How? I had no clue at first.

I took a shot. On the fly and with no time to undertake a thorough assessment, I premised from her memory that intense fears and dread were facilitating the sarcoidosis, probably by sapping and compromising her immune system, more than the reverse. So I said to her: "I applaud your courage in being willing to confront your fears. A hero is not someone who operates with no fear; a hero is someone who acts despite her fear. Your memory is telling me about your courage; you are afraid, and yet you remain to look ever more closely."

The Mind Affects the Body   51

She sighed, as if she had been understood—and probably at the challenge of the journey that lay ahead.

Her subsequent memories told me what she was afraid of, and we spent perhaps between 15 and 20 sessions talking about each situation, serially, and what about each made her afraid. Each situation was, metaphorically, a bug, a spider, a cobweb, and the like. As we finished each memory, a little more fear was processed and released. At the end of roughly three months, it was time for her to return to her pulmonary specialist, who was shocked to find she was still alive and able to keep her appointment.

But he was even more shocked after examining her to find she had no trace of sarcoidosis. She was "cured," however one might construe that word. She returned home elated: Death's executioner met and vanquished![1]

When we met next time, we talked about our sessions and what happened. My conclusion: I met a warrior and through memories work helped her to become an even more dynamic and effective warrior. I told her, "In my eyes you are a hero. You feared much when we began. You faced every fear, fought it to its knees, and emerged triumphant. I bow to you. You are truly a hero!" She returned to her life as a young wife and busy mother. I never heard from her again.

An important question: Were the fears in her memories *causing* the sarcoidosis? If so, what was the mechanism? Honestly? I can't say. My best guess would be that her fears, which preexisted her sarcoidosis, were flooding, overwhelming, and seriously compromising her immune system; the sarcoidosis emerged as an opportunistic, weakest link disease.

In my career I have treated patients with multiple sclerosis, various digestive disorders, a case of shingles that attacked the visual system threatening imminent blindness, cancers (including multiple myeloma), and many other medical problems. Although I never had much luck with arthritis, all my other patients recovered from their serious medical problems except a gentleman with an extremely aggressive strain of multiple myeloma who lived five years after diagnosis and through many cancer treatment protocols and died of the flu when he had to be taken off his cancer medications.

How do I explain this success? Again, I can't—not with any precision. But my best guess is the work done on psychological issues relieves strains on the immune system sufficiently that it can fight off the disease. Can anyone else do what I do effectively? Yes, absolutely. When I worked with prison inmates in groups using memories work (Chapter 11), the prison administration challenged me to demonstrate that someone else could do what I did and produce the outcomes they were seeing. I accepted the challenge and was successful. But perhaps the best evidence is the study DeMuth and I (1997) reported with a similar inmate population. It is the technique —memories work—that is efficacious, not the person (in this case, DeMuth, not me) who delivers the treatment.

52 *The Mind Affects the Body*

If Clients Change Their Behavior, Do Their Brains Change as Well?

Kandel (2006) has been a pioneer in his work with animal learning. His book, written after he won the Nobel Prize, should be required reading for mentalists, such as psychologists, who work with the mind and yet

old connections and laying down new, more adaptive connections for clients with emotional problems.

Note

1 How do physicians construct "miraculous cures" of the sort that occurred with my sarcoidosis patient? Mostly, they don't. They describe what happened as a spontaneous remission. Put plainly, I did nothing significant in their opinion except, perhaps, to be nice to a patient and spend time. After all, disease is disease is disease, as anyone knows, and only physicians treat diseases effectively. My response? Some day we will understand mind-body interactions with a lot more precision than we do now.

8 Writing Memories Down Without Discussing Them May Facilitate Understanding

For as long as I can remember, clinicians have debated whether we should ask clients to write down their memories or request them in session. At times, I have been on one or the other or both sides of the issue. I will sketch out the positions here.

I initially requested written memories from research subjects and transcribed patient memories in my clinical work, which I did for 13 years. Early on, I valued the flexibility of an oral procedure in clinical work. I wanted to explore matters in an inquiry that might be unclear in a written format. While flexibility is a clear advantage, there are disadvantages to oral procedures. One is writing down long memories in session and maintaining the mind-set of a clinician while functioning as a stenographer. I personally confess to problems multitasking, particularly with clients who spoke rapidly and had extensive memories. On the other hand, I trained psychologists who typed memories directly onto a computer notebook, and that worked for them. They were superb typists—very fast and accurate. I found the duality in their consciousness breathtaking as they typed away at 100 words per minute it seemed.

At the end of a clinical session, I dictated the protocols and my interpretations to my secretary before I forgot key information. Sometimes it took as much as 30 minutes to dictate a protocol. It was not unusual to have my secretary produce a seven-page single-spaced early memories document.

When we request memories in therapy as part of a verbal interaction, we initiate a process of distraction, intentional or not. Clients are commonly thinking about early memories, and they are also thinking about the interviewer's reaction to the information provided: "Am I doing this task properly? How is the doctor reacting to my memory? Am I providing too much/too little information?"

Writing down the memories in a quiet place facilitates a quasi-meditational process that enables the client to go deeper into the memory without the distraction of having to process the clinician's reactions. I discovered this by accident around 1985 as I began to experiment with early versions of the EMP. Initially my intent was to sample the whole

54   *Writing Memories Down*

of autobiographical memory, having established to my own satisfaction that the earliest childhood memory might not be as important to many clients as having lost a parent, having been molested, and so forth—often later memories. Then came questions about inter-judge reliability so, to make certain that the most important aspects of the memory were

when a standard administration EMP has been used, but tighter controls may need to be used in some legal cases.

How have I resolved the question of in-session transcription versus protocols written by the client?

I found most clients learned more about themselves when they wrote down their answers and were minimally distracted by their surroundings. Since my primary intent was to facilitate a better therapeutic outcome, I decided to create a procedure that would help me understand what brought my clients to therapy while it simultaneously helped them learn about themselves through the assessment experience. I designed the EMP to teach clients about memories-based insight-oriented therapy beginning around 1985. I wanted them to know more about what had brought them to this place in their life where they felt stuck and did not know how to move forward. By presenting useful tasks and raising thoughtful questions, the EMP led new clients through a structured life review. Most clients said they learned a great deal about themselves.

For those clients who were not particularly reflective, on the other hand, the EMP provided an opportunity to begin that process. Many clients initially considered memories as random stories from their past that meant "nothing." Perhaps they began remembering upsetting or traumatic events, but even on these occasions many clients had no idea how the past was connected to their present. For them, they were simply grateful that the past was "the past" and had absolutely nothing to do with their present psychological environment. It was at this point that the educational part of memories work began: "Perhaps these experiences

Writing Memories Down 55

are more relevant to you now than you previously thought. Perhaps you are noticing that the feelings you experienced in that memory are similar to feelings you have now when . . . What do you make of that?"

How do I introduce the EMP to new clients?

At the end of the initial visit I say something like this:

> Before we meet next time I would like you to complete this procedure (I put the EMP in their hands). *The Early Memories Procedure* will help me understand more about [the presenting problem which brought you in—depression, relationship issues, etc.]. I know that X [problem] is concerning for you, and I want you to get some relief as soon as possible. To make that happen I need to know more about your life experiences and how they have affected you, which might otherwise take many months. I use the EMP to speed things up. In the next week can you spend roughly three hours completing this procedure? [I rifle through the procedure as I talk.] There are six memories in Part I and 15 in Part II, and some questions that accompany. Many people do Part I in one sitting and Part II in a second sitting. Some find it easier to type their responses on computer. Can you set aside about three hours in the next week to complete this? If so, I promise I will read what you have written next time in session and share my thoughts with you. My goal is to finish next session with a much clearer idea of what is now causing you problems with X, and begin to address it. Is that a good plan for you?

I then set a second appointment to interpret.

Many clinicians who are new to memories work tell me they don't feel comfortable interpreting on the fly in the second session. If so, I suggest modifying the dialog to include a second session where you discuss the EMP experience in session and explore their reactions: "So, how did it feel to re-experience those events? What affected you the most? . . ." Before the third session, review and interpret the protocol. Focus especially on the clearest/most negative memory in Part I that will clarify what brought them into therapy (note EMP, p. 11 for "most significant memory" to provide a double check), whether they can tell you that or not. When you have identified that memory, in the interpretive session say something like this with the following sample interpretation: "I see in Memory 6, your clearest/most important memory lifetime, your mother died. You two were very close, you note, and you felt devastated when you lost her. It felt unfair, and you withdrew. You are now trying to figure out how to move on with your life. Do I have that right? And you do not know how to build a relationship that could even come close to replacing what you had with your mother. Is that right? And so it sounds like we need to explore in more detail what made her special and how you might begin to build elements like that into a current relationship.

56 *Writing Memories Down*

I know it won't be the same as it was with your mother, but it sounds like you would like to have someone to share with, someone who supports you in your endeavors. Have I missed something else that is really important to you?"

Clients who have never been in therapy before have little idea what can

to get much from it due to her many years of therapy. She completed the procedure. Her second early memory described how she was sexually molested by her second-grade teacher, whom she liked a lot before that event. She avoided being alone with the teacher after that. She could not tell her parents. She could not tell anybody. She had never told her therapist, not even after ten years. I asked her how it felt to tell me. There was a long pause. "I could never have told you either but you asked me to write it down. It would have been too embarrassing otherwise." That was where she was stuck in her life—she could not talk about things that embarrassed or upset her. This created a formality and distance she could not see that permeated her personal relationships. Although we did not have a therapy relationship—she was writing an article about what I did—I suggested she begin with telling her parents. This was part of a therapy process I call "finding your voice" and entitling yourself to speak up. Many people—even very successful, well-functioning people—have not learned to connect with otherwise trusted people in their lives deeply enough that they can share experiences like this. As a result, limitations are put on current relationships that should have been worked out in childhood relationships. Once she shared with her parents—who were appalled at what had happened—she was able to discuss what happened with her analyst and begin to build life skills that had been stunted previously as a result of her being molested.

Once I developed the EMP, I observed that many clients were mired down in various relationships they had in the past—with their mother or father or even their current romantic partner (spouse). These problems were often evident in "a memory of Mother" or "a memory of Father" in the EMP or simply by self-report as they mulled over their EMPs. Accordingly, I developed *Memories of mother* (Bruhn, 1993c), *Memories of father* (Bruhn, 1993b) and *Memories of spouse* (Bruhn, 1993d) to explore these relationships in greater detail. *The romantic relationships procedure* (Bruhn, 1989b) was designed to help clients who had problems establishing or maintaining emotionally intimate relationships. It will not come as a surprise that many of us import dysfunctional patterns from our relationships with our mothers or fathers to primary relationships in our lives as adults. The intent of these procedures, which are used as needed, is to telescope what the problem is so that it can be discussed and unwound in session. One problem with therapy is that it often takes a very long time for clients to develop a perspective about their lives, and lacking that, it is very difficult for them to build the motivation to make changes in their lives or even to understand why they need to. Early in my career I found myself at the end of a session often muttering sub-vocally, "If they could only see things as I see them."

Now they can.

These memory procedures provide the tools to develop a perspective about present circumstances that might otherwise require years of therapy. Am I saying that completing memories procedures substitutes for therapy? No. There is a difference between better understanding what the problem is and fixing the problem. For most people, therapy is still necessary. If we could see ourselves as clearly as our most perceptive friends and colleagues see us, however, we could resolve many of our problems and get our lives on track by ourselves.

But we can't, most of us anyway. Which is where memory procedures enter the picture.

9 "Instant Cures" in "Therapy"

can be challenging and progress slow. Just such a case involved a brilliant man on disability who discovered in adulthood he had a life challenging problem with bi-polar 2, likely precipitated by alcohol abuse. Substance abuse destroyed his career and resulted in several incarcerations. I undertook memories work with him, beginning with an EMP. When things were at their worst, he was drinking two bottles of wine a day or more. When they were better as treatment progressed, he maintained sobriety for 30 days or more. His treatment involved confronting multiple traumatic memories—some in childhood, some later. Each trauma needed to be addressed. This case is presented in more detail in the Case Study at the end of this book and offers a more detailed look at what often happens in cases where complex memories work is needed.

We know change can dramatically occur in an instant. But how does it happen?

The key memory in a series commonly incorporates a "load-bearing structure" that, once identified and modified, can cause critical elements in the personality to transform and "flip." What seems to be a minor change from a psychological perspective can be profound and transformational from an engineering perspective.

Example 1

Consider the example of the patient in Chapter 4 who struggled with this contextual issue when her therapist was about to leave for vacation: "When I am about to be abandoned and express my apprehension and anxieties, I expect not to be heard."

"Instant Cures" in "Therapy" 59

How to take this structure down? In this case, it took one session. What was done? I listened. She was heard. I did not abandon her. I assured her that I thought her therapist could hear her also. That reassurance held her over, and her therapist, an extremely competent professional, talked her through her feelings after he returned from vacation.

The memory of being attacked by guard dogs depicted in metaphor what kept her from connecting more deeply to people she depended on and loved who also cared for her. Once she was able to identify the source of her anxieties and release them, she could talk with her therapist about connecting, her fears about same, and her anxieties about dependency and loss. The impasse was broken. She could move forward. Did I "cure" her in one session? No. I identified where in her memory she was stuck, broke up the primary "constriction," and she returned to her therapist where she continued her work.

Let's look at another example.

Example 2

I used to be a decent athlete and an average ballplayer. A wonderful friend who played basketball as it should be played was signed by a South American team after his college eligibility ended. He wrote to me and told me he could get a place for me on the team if I came down. I liked "Fred," who was the older brother I never had. We both loved jazz, loved to party, and loved the game, but it had been a while since I played. What the heck, I decided to fly down and give it a shot. I was 20 years old at the time, I had just finished my undergraduate degree, and the travel part appealed.

There was hardly a week that Fred did not make the newspaper. We North Americans lit up the night and raised the sun. The hot spots in the city knew us by our first names. It was great fun for a young man who had just turned 21.

By the time I left the team in mid-1963 with chronic amoebic dysentery, and 75 pounds lighter, it was clear to me that Fred had a drinking problem. Shoot, *I* had a drinking problem. Who was I kidding?

The two of us kept in touch. In those days, we wrote. After I got married in 1967, I pledged to my wife to stop drinking—complete sobriety. I knew I was spending a lot of money on beer, not to mention a lot of time consuming it in local taverns. I also knew intuitively that I would soon have to choose between drinking and my marriage if I did not stop. Incredibly, I kept my word for many years.

Meanwhile, Fred continued his basketball career and played with the Chilean national team. In due time he hung up his sneaks and came back to the States. He settled near his wife's family and scrambled to get a job in a cosmopolitan Southern city, which remained highly segregated and deeply racist. He finally found a position teaching Spanish and Russian at a black high school. He slowly broke into coaching.

60 *"Instant Cures" in "Therapy"*

He did what he could—coached girls' teams after Title IX and fresh-man and junior varsity boys' teams. He wrote to tell me his teams went undefeated for years. He took his Spanish classes to Mexico for spring breaks to practice their Spanish. He sent literally dozens of his kids to Division 1 colleges on full athletic scholarships. Fred could teach. Fred

the team.

By this visit I had been doing memories work over ten years with my private patients in Bethesda. After practice Fred and I talked about what I was doing with memories. Why memories, he wondered? I asked him, rather than explain the process: "What is your earliest memory?"

"You mean of drinking?" he laughed.

"Not necessarily. Just your earliest memory."

"Funny you should ask," he replied. My mother's boyfriend took me into a club when I was two years old, sat me on the bar and bought me a shot of whiskey. Probably thought I'd try to drink it and spit it out. Good for a laugh. I downed it neat as could be! He looked shocked. I'll never forget the look on his face. He bought me another one. I threw that down too. It was pretty good. The entire bar came over to see this little kid who could throw down shots of whiskey like he knew what he was doing. I felt special!"[1]

"Huh!" I said. "Now I get it. You think you are special because of how much you can drink, right?"

"That's right! Can't no man drink more than I do," he said, proudly. "I can drink anyone under the table!"

"I've got a big surprise for you, Fred."

He looked at me skeptically like I was setting him up for a con.

"People like and respect you despite your drinking. The people who really love and respect you appreciate that you teach Spanish and Russian with passion. That you take your kids to Mexico for spring break to practice their Spanish. That you coach like a master, teach your kids to love the game and play it right. Your kids would die for you. You pick out a wall for them to run through. There they go! They respect that you have gotten dozens of your players into college on scholarships, and that you have taught boys from poor single-parent homes by your example what a man is. That's why they love and respect you. Not because of how much you drink."

Fred looked at me, speechless and stunned. He never even considered the importance of all his other accomplishments, which he generally dismissed as nothing very much. It was just what he did. His enduring claim to fame, as he figured it, was his ability to hold his liquor. Fred was an extremely competitive individual. Now that his playing career was over, and athletic competition behind him, his drinking career began in earnest—that's how I was seeing his earliest memory.

He told me later he enrolled in AA for the first time and began a treatment program. This one conversation did not completely unwind 50-plus years of drinking, but I believe it I believe it initiated the process that enabled Fred to finally see himself as strong and worthy of respect but not alcoholic.

Fred stopped drinking New Year's Day, 1995. He has not had a drink since, 23 years later. He is now as proud of his many years of sobriety as he was of his ability to drink anyone under the table. Every year I try to send him a box of steaks to celebrate his abstinence.

Memories are powerful in part because they can point us to where change needs to take place and what might happen if it does.

Example 3

Joe was referred for anxiety and depression.

A cop, Joe was in the middle of a major legal problem. An expert marksman, he was called to a hostage situation where the very pregnant girlfriend of a notorious drug dealer was being held in their home with a gun to her head. The situation was dramatic and chaotic. Was the hostage taker high on something? Quite possibly. Backed against a wall, he was surrounded by a small mob of police and authorities with belligerent threats and counter threats flying back and forth. Media were in the background, camera flashes going off. Thirty minutes went by, the tension constantly ratcheting. Joe looked to get a clear shot with his sidearm. Way too dangerous.

Finally, he saw the tiniest of openings for a clear shot. A head shot. He took it. The hostage's life and her baby's saved!

62 *"Instant Cures" in "Therapy"*

That's when Joe's drama really began. Joe was charged with killing the hostage taker. The department investigated the shooting. He was cleared. Then, ironically, he was sued by the hostage for shooting her boyfriend. Another long, complex and highly publicized trial followed.

That was the immediate basis for Joe's anxiety and depression, and

His father continued to drink. But he did so quietly. No more threats, no more beatings. There was a new sheriff in town.

This was my comment to Joe: "Someone had to put a stop to the crap that was going on in your house. That someone was you."

I went on: "You had the chance to be your father and beat the bejesus out of him as he had beaten you so many times before. But you didn't. 'Vengeance is mine,' saith the Lord. You chose the alternative—stop the violence."

With that, his anxiety and depression began to remit. Until then he saw his father as an oppressive force in his life and not himself as a man who took charge in crises and did the right thing.

I told Joe:

> We cannot control what a judge or jury will decide. In my book you deserve a medal. I trust your reporting. The department has exonerated you. But we don't know what a jury will decide. We have to let that go. Here is what we know: Just as you acted with your father, you did what you had to do as a cop. You stopped the violence. The outcome? You know what the truth is. Pray that this will turn out for the best and go on with your life.

After a long trial, Joe was found not at fault. In that situation Joe found out who his friends were. But he held his head high, as he should, no matter what the outcome, and went on to lead an extremely productive life.

There was a new sheriff in town. He was a fair and just man.

Whatever his father's actions and choices were based on, Joe built his own foundation. We continued to process and reorganize the sequelae of what happened, which flowed from his new self-perception.

Example 4

I began working with Joan in crisis. She had been seriously dating a man for some time and was entrenched in an intensely abusive relationship. Alexander was handsome, wealthy, well educated, and both verbally and physically abusive to a deeply disturbing extent. There were threats, condemnations, vilifications, and physical abuse. From the first session I was extremely alarmed and told Joan she was at risk. She had to file a police report and stop seeing Alexander until we could sort out what was happening.

Many therapists would focus exclusively on this abusive relationship and count their intervention as successful if their client survived and did not immediately begin another abusive relationship. On one level I would not disagree.

However, it bothered me that Joan's psychic alarm system seemed to be completely shut off. She did not respond to a danger that most of us would immediately register.

I gave her an EMP. Her clearest most negative memory was being punished by her father, a prominent and very successful man who was admired by everyone in his community as a God-like figure. In the memory she was four years old, and her father came home early from work. He accused her of doing something wrong, something very minor as close as I could tell. Her punishment was to kneel in front of the toilet on the hard ceramic tiles for two hours, without crying. She was terrified. Her knees were killing her. But she shut up. She was too afraid to complain or speak up. She loved her father, as everyone did, but she was afraid to talk with him.

I told her, "I am seeing your father in Alexander. You never learned to speak up to your father when there was a problem. You could not defend yourself. You assumed the problem must be you. Have I got it right?" She agreed. "Alexander is not your father. I am afraid that he will hurt you. This is a dangerous relationship. Can you stop seeing him and put limits on what he is doing?" She did.

Once Alexander was out of the picture, I focused on her family. Did her mother know what had happened when she was four years old? Did she tell her? No, she hadn't. Gradually, I encouraged her to find her voice and learn to speak up and set limits. Without being able to maintain limits, she would continue to be at risk in relationships. She reconnected with her mother and began to confide in her. Much later in the process,

64 *"Instant Cures" in "Therapy"*

when things were safer, I urged her to talk to her father about her memory. Did he remember that? He did. He was ashamed and remorseful. He had been too ashamed to talk with her. What prompted this incident to occur was that he was going through a deeply challenging time at work. He felt angry and out of control. What he did was wrong, he said. He

she developed the skills she needed, she began to date men who were more centered and less like her father at a time when he was functioning poorly in his professional life. When he died, much later in our work, his passing took place after many heartfelt conversations filled with mutual appreciation. His passing was mourned by hundreds of people in his work community whose lives his wisdom and compassion had touched.

Without knowing the memories that generate significant dysfunctional patterns in our clients, we often move from one crisis to another with a new Alexander trailing in the footsteps of the last, never seeing the template in the memory that is producing this cascade of troubles that accumulates in our office.

Example 5

I will offer one of my own memories, which was taken from self-therapy, as an example.

I come from a wonderful family. I was an only child, much valued by my parents, both of whom had suffered losses of beloved siblings in their youth. I was therefore doubly special to them. And they loved each other immensely, as much, certainly, as any parents I knew about. That loving and settled family experience has remained with me through my life and has been my most enduring and foundational life experience: To be loved and to love in return.

"Instant Cures" in "Therapy" 65

My father was a naval officer who had the soul of a poet and actor but the duty assignment at the end of his career of an accountant responsible for the payroll of the U.S. Navy for the eastern United States. "To the penny," as he used to tell me. He balanced the books dutifully, and I recall his flying to Washington every month from Cleveland for stressful budget meetings. In his youth he was a competent athlete, a cowboy, a martial arts practitioner, a journalist, and a salesman. Although the summation of these parts rarely meshes seamlessly in a single human being, he somehow managed to cobble it together.

At age 17, I enrolled in the School of Engineering at the University of Portland, where I did ok. My German mathematics professor, whom I liked and respected, told me that I was on track to become a successful engineer. Which seemed entirely possible. But I also had a fantasy to be a discus thrower. While my fellow engineering students were hitting their books, I went to the gym on my own for three hours each afternoon and lifted weights like a man possessed. Although I was nearly 6 foot 7 inches, I weighed only 170 pounds as a freshman. I was not nearly strong enough to compete collegiately. By the end of my first year, I added 55 pounds of pure muscle. I went to our A.D. and asked for a track scholarship, which I got with no hesitation. Perhaps it was the 18-inch biceps.

Beginning sophomore year, I was told by my engineering advisor that I needed to take some liberal arts courses to fulfill my degree requirements. I had an opening in my schedule first thing in the morning for an Introduction to Psychology class.

The first lecture was on personality; I was riveted. I was transported to another reality. The lecture was on helping people with emotional problems. That's how I remember it at least.

In that lecture I was transfixed. That is what I would do! I would become a clinical psychologist, and I would help people. I had no idea at all how that would happen, but it was as if I had been hit by lightning. In that lecture, at that moment, I knew my future. That would be my life. I never had a second thought.

I changed majors to psychology and decided that I would go to Harvard to do my doctoral work. I had no idea what Harvard offered. I just knew by osmosis that if I went there I could learn what I needed.

That one lecture was all I needed to reach a final decision about my career choice. I knew I wanted to help people and that clinical psychology would be my chosen profession. I also profoundly understood I was an 18-year-old college sophomore who did not have enough life experience to help myself, let alone anyone else. So I studied, I lifted weights, I threw the discus, and later I played basketball in South America. These oddly cobbled-together life goals never bothered me for a nanosecond. Only later could I see that each dream was real, each was true, and I was to learn something distinct and vital from each experience, including

66   *"Instant Cures" in "Therapy"*

my time in the School of Engineering. Despite the remarkable paucity of planning or practical experience, clinical psychology was indeed my life path.

The skeptic might think, "There had to be more to this than one psychology lecture, however amazing it might have been."

muscular build and severe anxiety did not fit together visually or psychologically. Unfortunately, I could do nothing. I knew nothing about how to fix a broken person, no matter how I cared about him as my friend.

Years later, at my request, my father bought me Freud's complete works before I went to graduate school at Duke. Unfortunately, Freud did not help me understand how to fix Ray's problem either, which is not surprising. The analytic system is designed to identify what is wrong, not how to fix what went wrong. Only in the 1980s, as I began to work on autobiographical memory theory and think about Ray in greater detail, did I begin to understand where Ray was caught. He was a victim of trauma by his parents, who were supposed to support him emotionally, not torture him. Ray had an issue with trust: "If people who are supposed to love me the most do things like this to me, who can I trust?" His anxiety was borne of a profound suspicion about people. He continued to expect that terrible things would happen to him for nothing. And despite looking like the last person in a bar you would ever pick a fight with, he remained chronically fearful. I should add Ray was a really nice person. Reserved and a wary, true, but not mean or threatening at all. Sensitive and kind.

What did I learn from this part of my own self-analysis? I learned I wanted to help people initially because of Ray and our friendship. I knew what happened to him was profoundly wrong. But I also knew then that I did not have a clue as to what to do. The damage was done. Ray was broken. The police at that time would never respond to a complaint from a teenager. And even if I had reported this, the horses were out of the barn and far down the road. So, when I went to the psychology lecture about helping people with emotional problems, Ray's drama was resurrected by a ghost narrator in my unconscious who called me to action to become a clinical psychologist. It was a eureka moment. Put in words, it would sound something like, "Someone must do something." For me, Ray's trauma lent flesh and bones and a personal reality to my need to be helpful, to assist others who had not experienced my own good fortune in life.

Unwittingly, Ray became my first object lesson about how trauma can really mess people up. Had I been working in the 1990s with Ray professionally I would have condemned what happened to him; noted how he had become a body builder to protect himself now, to give a visual warning to would be abusers; and told him that anyone who tried to traumatize him now would have to be insane. That is head stuff though. We needed to consider how to heal his past. The best idea that came to me was for him to talk to kids in schools about his experiences and how to protect themselves. He would have been fabulous in that role as a body builder. But it took years for me to create memories work and develop an approach to work with damaged clients.

As I looked at the problem through the perspective of what I learned subsequently, I realized that Ray would have needed an action-oriented approach to therapy, one focused on correcting the damage, something that mirrored the process of body building work. But how to do that? The answer that came was the following: Ray understood "doing" very well; he needed to engage in "undoing." That would be the most potent dynamic for him, and for many traumatized patients. The doing, in his case, was being scalded and tortured. The undoing might be talking to schoolchildren about trauma they experience, such as being bullied or excessive, inappropriate punishment, while getting clear in his own neurology exactly how he should have been treated, and repeating that many times while trying to help others avoid what he suffered. This kind of repetition would mirror what he had done as a bodybuilder. Doing set after set to get better.

Would that have "cured him" of his trauma? No. He would always remember what happened. But he would improve his coping skills, along with limits and boundaries. As would the kids he worked with.

With appreciation to Freud, I acknowledge the role of unconscious motivation and how it impacts life choices. It certainly affected my life choice—I don't think I have ever been more upset by anything than I was by Ray's punishment memories. Ray was brutally abused by parents who should have provided a nurturing environment, not abused him. For me, the experience of that memory, even while it remained unconscious, was life altering. It depicted the psychological inverse of my parents and my relationship with them—it went beyond shocking.

It was also a load-bearing memory. I wanted to help others who had been hurt. I could not at the time—only later.

68 *"Instant Cures" in "Therapy"*

Ray's trauma was a core recollection from self-therapy I did with myself. Was I the first to adopt this type of self-analysis? No. Freud's book on dreams (1899/1913) reflects an intense process of self-analysis as he worked with his own repressed memories. Carl Jung (1963) was also intensely moved by working with his early memories:

introduced me to trauma I never experienced in my own life and pushed me to think about how such memories could be re-engineered and their templates reconfigured to provide relief to those who suffer emotionally. But the final twist is also important: While I personally had never been traumatized as Ray had, I was traumatized by proxy, which was sufficient to open me up emotionally to the undergraduate psychology lecture I experienced. However good it was, the lecture did not convince me to become a psychologist. My connection with Ray, and the bond we shared, set my course, which has made all the difference.

I appreciate what Ray taught me then, and I understand, odd though it might sound, that though our high school connection Ray became my first trauma teacher. Else, I would have very likely become an engineer and not experienced the passion my life choice has created.

Example 6

Seth was referred by a former client for relational issues. A handsome, well-educated man, Seth was generally perceived as "the world's nicest guy." He was very generous in relationships and easily attracted the interest of a number of beautiful women. His relationships had a long duration, but he seemed unable to commit, and each relationship in turn eventually failed. He was stuck in a very sad pattern.

I gave Seth an EMP. When he finally found time to complete it, he called and thanked me for what I had done for him. He said that the EMP

"Instant Cures" in "Therapy" 69

changed his life, he figured out what was wrong, and now he was ready to move on. He was very appreciative.

Several years later, he called again and made a new appointment. He thanked me for the prior help I had given him, which set me back a bit because, although Seth had filled out the EMP, we hadn't talked about what he reported.

"What was helpful?" I asked

It was hard for him to describe beyond it was a particular memory he wrote down. "Which one?" I asked.

It was Memory 6, a later life memory. He was at work in the middle of something timely and critical in his professional life. A work crisis. His mother was phoning him urgently. Why? She was shopping at Neiman Marcus, had bought a lot of clothes, and needed him to pick her up and take her home. He tried to explain that he was at work. He couldn't come. How about a cab? He would pay for it. No, she said, she needed *him*. He came.

The memory reminded him that he was at his mother's beck and call. Of all his siblings, he was the only one she called. He had many memories with the same form. Some involved his father as well. His parents were divorced.

Now he knew why.

He began by putting limits on this relationship. She called with another demand. He loved her, yes, but he could not come now. Perhaps another time. He was at work.

By degrees he created a reasonable distance and independence. He found his voice. He entitled himself to say no. He set limits which, before, he thought were incompatible with loving someone. How could you love someone and say "no"?

His mother was not happy with his new independence, but she accepted it. Previously, she had done so with his other siblings.

As we gained traction on his relationship with his mother, we began to look at his relationships with girlfriends and fiancées over the years. Previously, he had been ashamed to explore these in any depth. Now we saw why. He realized he needed to set limits but hadn't because he was afraid he would be rejected. He could now see he was loved. He no longer had to be in each interaction the nicest guy in the world.

He had been dating a beautiful woman for seven years, but he could not make a commitment. I wondered why.

He described a series of events that left him with the clear message that she needed to be first and foremost in his life, and, if she wasn't, she would quickly be dating other men. Her needs were extensive and time consuming. Her background revealed she had been married to a demanding, abusive man, and to her credit she was looking to break free from that pattern. Unfortunately, their needs were conflicting, as Seth

70 *"Instant Cures" in "Therapy"*

was looking to break free from a pattern of being the polar opposite to her ex-husband. His mother was much too close in personality to his girl-friend. Although she was happy with the old Seth, the new Seth needed a relationship based more on mutuality where he did not have to be the personal servant or caretaker of his partner.

tion and not spend a lot of time he didn't have at a gym. As his stress level fell as he exercised, his desire to drink also declined, and he was able to shift to non-alcoholic beer when he went out with friends. Then we did an EMP.

His key memory involved wanting to be the best at school while being raised by a divorced mother in a lower middle-class family of at most average achievers. Roger had several siblings who were not academically oriented. He locked himself into his room every day after school and studied until he fell asleep. He took his meals in his room. By the most microscopic margin he edged out a very worthy competitor in his class and was named valedictorian. He achieved his objective, was accepted by a good school, and won a scholarship. He presented as a serious, deter-mined, goal-oriented individual who was willing to pay the price for the extraordinary level of achievement he desired. The next question was, what reward did he deserve for this level of achievement?

His second key memory took place post-college graduation after he began to work. His mother was going through bankruptcy from chronic overspending. He took over her finances and paid off her debt with her promise to repay. His mother reneged on her agreement, did not pay him, and called the police on him on a trumped-up charge. He was found guilty and sentenced to jail. Complete betrayal. The gist of the memory was that he opted to become a good Samaritan, was betrayed and victim-ized. Emotionally, he was left for dead.

His was a challenging situation to process in therapy. I emphasized that he did the right thing. His mother was in distress. He helped her out

"Instant Cures" in "Therapy"   71

over and beyond what most people would expect. Ironically, after he paid her debt off, in six months she was back to where she was before he bailed her out. We agreed he would cut her off and let cause and effect play out as there was nothing else he could do without having the police re-enter the picture. Meanwhile, he could work on his own finances. I suggested that he call his father, whom he had not spoken to in years, for his perspective. His father told him enough that he realized he had not been the first person on his mother's dance card. Unlike what happened with his studies, I noted that sometimes we do our very best and things do not work out. We cannot control what other people do after we do what we commit to do.

At work he continued to pour his energies into a project that would literally change history. The media consensus was that his goal would never be achieved. As he made progress on his goal, things at work unfortunately took a major turn for the worse. A problem emerged with an employee. His version of events differed substantially from hers. He had never had a problem like this before. Although he was not fired, his authority was restricted. The scenario reminded me of what had happened with his mother when he did nothing wrong but ended up in jail. He agreed. Incredibly, his project continued to progress, and I read about his successes monthly in the *Washington Post* and witnessed them on TV. Through Roger's diligence an entirely new business was created that employed hundreds of thousands of people.

What was the tipping point in Roger's drama? I think it was accepting he could do his best and win, and still, on a near-term basis, not succeed as he intended through no fault of his own. Although he did become valedictorian and win a college scholarship, he also did the "right thing" with his mother after he began working and ended up in jail. He failed not because he did not do enough but because he was not dealing with someone who appreciated what he offered and reciprocated. His mother had a compulsive spending addiction, and he became ensnared in it.

Even though he changed the world through his professional work, the most he could do in his personal life was to let his mother go and not continue to be revictimized. From his history with his mother, he was left with a deep mistrust of women, which caused him to create an emotional distance in romantic relationships even when that was not needed. He vainly continued to search for someone strong enough to take care of herself that he could trust in an emotionally satisfying relationship.

Unfortunately, memories work does not guarantee a Hollywood ending. Roger achieved extraordinary success in his work, but his intimate relationships continued to be a challenge as he processed the emotional devastation that his mother visited upon him. I pointed out that while he did his best to "fix" his mother, she refused to be fixed.

72 *"Instant Cures" in "Therapy"*

What was the load-bearing memory here? There were two operating together. Doing the best he could academically and winning while following the same pattern at work with even more success. But despite being judged "the best," not being able to save his mother from her spending addiction and instead being betrayed. He eventually accepted

in romantic relationships persisted. As I see it, the trauma with his mother ran very deep. It was difficult for Roger to give up his attraction for "handless maidens" like his mother who needed to be rescued as these women needed him tremendously and made him feel strong and capable. Which can become another kind of addiction unfortunately.

Therapy with mis-connection issues like Roger's, once other matters ameliorate, sometimes require several relational cycles to correct. The ultimate desired outcome requires patience.

Example 8

We have been identifying load-bearing memories that play a key role in self-regulation and in perceiving the world. But what happens when there are multiple problematic memories, many of which are active simultaneously?

I am personally most challenged in my clinical work by cases in which there are substantial gaps in a client's early life experiences, often caused by an extended illness, loss of a significant other, or a failure to experience an emotionally safe, secure environment. Therapists commonly struggle when the pattern of a client's early life resembles Swiss cheese, with critical experiences missing entirely. These gaps often culminate in many dysfunctional memories, following the principle that the mind needed something missing in order to operate properly.

Milton Erickson once treated an individual with huge gaps in her autobiographical memories via what I would describe as a workaround

"Instant Cures" in "Therapy" 73

"patch." Haley (1973) titled Erickson's case "The February Man." About to be married, a young woman turned to Erickson for help. She came from a wealthy family where she was raised by a succession of minimally involved household staff while her parents were busy with endless social obligations. Now on the eve of her wedding, she felt completely unprepared to be a wife or mother. She had no memories of family experiences to draw upon as she was about to enter into this new phase of life. What to do?

Erickson, surprisingly, chose to hypnotize her and program her with what he surmised to be the emotional aspects of the memories she was missing at that time in her youth. Enter the February Man, a psychological stand-in, who came to visit each year, arriving with great interest and emotional support, always glad to see her, share her adventures from the previous year and build upon them now. Why February? Nothing much happened in her life in February, so the chances of interfering with the memory of an important experience in her existing memory system were minimized. The February Man provided her emotionally with what she had never received from her parents and household staff. That done, Erickson suggested she forget the specifics of the memories they created and remember only the feeling of the experience. At the end of a brief hypnotherapy, the patient told Erickson she recalled nothing they had worked on but felt ready to move on with her life and get married. Thus ended one of the more challenging and creative treatments in brief psychotherapy.

My accidental homage to Erickson follows.

When I was a newly minted psychologist, a man who was to become a brilliant film producer presented with crippling anxiety. Unwittingly, he introduced me to load-bearing memories and their resolution.

Jim had a history of early losses and from these, sketchy life experiences and deficient people skills. There was no one available to teach him. Now as an adult he suffered through life as a psychological and actual orphan. On the surface he presented as a perfectionist who could not make decisions. Why? He wasn't sure about "this," and he didn't know "that." How to proceed? Jim was having a terrible time, and frankly I was not meeting my own expectations as a helper. I was willing, but his was looking more and more like a lifetime case of having to explain the obvious and make connections until things finally came together for him in frustratingly small chunks. His memories revealed a bewildering variety of anxiety and depression generators. I did my best, but for every problem we reduced in size, there were two more impatiently tugging from the wings for his attention.

Unexpectedly, Jim was given an opportunity to fly to Paris, which he loved. A possible funding source emerged for a film idea that had great promise. He decided, with trepidation, to fly to France and meet with the potential funder.

74 *"Instant Cures" in "Therapy"*

I awaited the outcome with similar trepidation. There were a variety of ways this trip could fail ingloriously, and each possibility came with its own painful consequences.

Jim returned greatly encouraged. Before leaving, he had been deeply depressed.

could even inquire in his peer group about certain technical and procedural aspects of filmmaking.

Whereas before, Jim was tied up in knots emotionally, he could now ask anyone literally anything. He was a tourist at home in DC. His mood shifted 180 degrees from anxious, depressed, and inhibited to confident, transparent, and friendly. He had assigned himself a new role in his own personal life movie. He had solved his own problem!

Just as important, he gave me a valuable tool to help similarly situated clients: "Be a tourist!" aka, "It is perfectly acceptable in certain situations to know nothing."

Only later did it occur to me that I helped set the stage, completely unwittingly, for him to invent "the tourist" by patiently answering what seemed like endless questions in therapy about life, people, and troublesome situations without criticism or judgment. From an odd perspective I was reborn as Jim's "February Man" or something close to it. I had become "the explainer."

Jim quickly found financial backing for his important documentary, organized the project, shot the movie, and sold it. It was a wonderful film that won many awards.

Jim taught me an important lesson. He discovered that he was making himself miserable by expecting much more from himself than others did. He therefore decided to lower the bar. Most people can identify with an underdog. He presented a minimal threat and needed a lot of help. In Jim's case, the secret was to admit to knowing little and to let others teach him what he needed to learn. By accepting that role, Jim bypassed a daunting set of memories by changing his process in situations he found threatening. He invented his own workaround.

Let's return to the concept of *load-bearing memory*. What was the load-bearing memory? In retrospect I see a consolidation of several memories: "I lost X who died; I lost Y who left me" and so forth. What underlying structure we were working on? As I see it: "I have no one I can count on to answer my questions about life. I have been *orphaned*." As his therapist, I acted as the constant who listened to his questions about life and shared his struggles to find answers. Finally, he had an opportunity to leave for a time the small bit of comfort and security he had created and go to Paris. How could he get answers there?

He could be a tourist. What did he take from therapy? There might be satisfying answers to his questions if he found friendly looking people and gave them a chance to step up. Structurally, we needed to create the inverse of being orphaned—connecting with people.

Conclusions

Load-bearing memories may be the first (Fred's) or a later memory (Joe's, mine). They may be extremely negative (Joan's, Ray's), positive (Fred's), or simply very vivid (Joe's). They are commonly identified in the EMP as "the most important memory" (p. 11). Usually, they are also rated as exceptionally clear (spotlighted) in the EMP (pp. 9–10). In my therapeutic process with Jim, a workaround was needed to bypass holes in his developmental history which left him feeling paralyzed and inadequate. In retrospect, I see I was working with a repeating memory about loss with the underlying form, "I have no one I can count on to answer the questions I have about life."

In an assessment, I begin with the most important memory in the protocol. Often, it is the clearest/most negative memory, but it may be simply a particularly clear memory, as was my own (lecture). In each case, I begin working to alter the template in that memory, which depicts what is not working for the client. Once the template changes, the personality reorganizes to incorporate that change. In my own memory, there was no template to change—I just wanted to understand what made the lecture so powerful that in that moment the entire course of my life was changed. From another perspective, what traumatized me was not knowing how to remediate a problem like Ray's. His experience permanently altered the trajectory of my professional life because of my concern for him.

After doing memories work on myself, I understood that my deepest motivation was to help those heal who had been terribly wounded by life. However, I was very young, had skipped ahead two grades, and needed life experiences and professional training to be helpful to others. My memory spotlighted what I wanted to accomplish. After I played basketball in South America, worked as an agency social worker (ADC),

76 *"Instant Cures" in "Therapy"*

obtained a teaching certificate, taught for six years in the public schools, learned computer programming, completed two master's degrees, got married, and had my first child—then and only then did I wake up one morning (literally) and feel I had enough life experience to help people. I was accepted as a 30-year-old graduate student at Duke, which was a

10 A Scoring System Is Needed to Categorize Autobiographical Memories

When the most general meaning is applied, a *taxonomy* is a scheme of classification. A Rorschach scoring system commonly describes a functional and descriptive taxonomy. There are several types of Rorschach responses—including human or animal responses. Depending on the scoring system, different features may be emphasized. Various Rorschach scoring systems name and classify types of responses.

In contrast to Rorschach responses, many important taxonomic differences among memories have largely gone unrecognized. The prevailing attitude has been, memories are memories are memories. Why do we need to categorize recollections of historic events? They actually happened. Rorschach responses did not happen. There are no butterflies, people beating drums, etc.

Rorschach responses are considered perceptions. Therefore, we are not surprised by scoring categories or taxonomic features of Rorschach responses.

We reflect, speaking broadly, that there is history, observable and verifiable, and then there are perceptions of that history. As Bergson suggested, we select events that we retain on a continuum of usefulness. The junk is thrown away and forgotten; the significant remains. But what, indeed, does a "taxonomy" of memories involve?

As we have seen, there are positive affect memories, negative affect memories, single events, and repeated events. There are also family memories, group identity memories (by religion, gender, ethnic origin, etc.), and several others, including false memories. There are spontaneous and directed memories, and multiply classified memories with process and content themes, such as spontaneous vs directed *punishment* memories (Bruhn, 1982a, 1982b). The variety in types of memories by itself suggests the need for a taxonomy or classification scheme. Let me suggest the beginning of such a scheme here (see Table 10.1).

78 *Categorizing Autobiographical Memories*

Table 10.1 A Taxonomy of Memory Variables Relevant to a Clinical Population

I Spontaneous Memories
   A Negative Affect (score: content or process theme)
   B Positive Affect (score: content or process theme)
   C Clarity (psychic energy spotlighting the memory)

like this."

3   Gender identification memories. Such memories tell us how the subject (S) perceives gender in his or her life.
4   Group identification memories. A memory may focus on religion, ethnic, regional, or national origin; or membership in a particular group the S has identified with.
5   False memories. Something the S previously believed is true but later found out was not.

Exner's Comprehensive System (1974) led to major advances with the Rorschach. It has been similarly proposed that a scoring system may help us better understand memories (Last & Bruhn, 1991) and how they function.

In the early 1980s Jeff Last and I believed that Early Memories needed its own scoring system similar to Exner's (1974) with the Rorschach. In 1983 Last proposed the *Comprehensive Early Memories Scoring System*. A few years later I realized that a section on content and process themes was needed, and the *Comprehensive Early Memories Scoring System—Revised* ensued (Last & Bruhn, 1991). Content and Process themes (Section VII) offer an easy entry into a powerful system used to sort experiences likely to have psychological significance to human beings. Where were these themes derived? Primarily through clinical observations with clients as we worked with material from their EMP protocols. Once I was convinced that these themes were used to filter and reorganize experience in real time, I realized that I had discovered a key element in the mental programming that was used to construct "useful" memories. For instance, if successful mastery—a key content theme—was featured in a set of memories, I knew that my client was oriented to mastery situations. If he was successful now, chances are he would be satisfied; if unsuccessful, he would be frustrated. Sounds fairly straightforward. But not all people are attracted to mastery situations; some gravitate to situations where they can connect and feel accepted and affirmed. The content and process themes in Section VII provided information on what is important to the client based on their memories. The clearest/most negative memory was likely to depict what was causing the client to seek therapy. Content and process themes thus became central to memories work, and Section VII aggregated the material from the central processor used by autobiographical memory. When I trained students, I gave them a stack of memories and Section VII from the CEMSS-R (see Appendix A). I told them: "Read these memories, score them, and let's compare scoring notes tomorrow."

As I developed memories work, I scored stacks of memories until I could see the underlying structure of the memory. I found that positive affect memories focused on important needs. Negative affect memories required a précis: "When 'X' occurs, I expect 'Y' will follow." The précis revealed the context causing the client trouble.

In 1995 I became interested in the distribution of types of memories in a general outpatient clinical practice, and so I scored memories from a set of EMPs completed by my patients. In the late 1990s Richards, Bruhn, Lucente, and Casey (2015) undertook a reliability study of content and process themes in connection with a memories work module in a landmark National Institute of Drug Abuse (NIDA) study of recidivism in a population of female inmates with a history of substance-abuse-related crimes. Even with a limited amount of time to train to criteria, reliability was acceptable.

What is an example of a common clinical content theme? The most prevalent is a theme featuring illness, injury, or hospitalization. Such memories commonly convey concerns about vulnerability and whether others can be trusted to provide care that is needed.

What makes Section VII themes important?

We want to find out what brings clients into therapy. If an EM concerning an injury is described, the issue is feeling vulnerable and wondering whether others will be responsive to their needs. There is a tension around that issue, which may be relatively minor or central to any therapeutic relationship they establish with us. Speaking metaphorically and literally,

80 *Categorizing Autobiographical Memories*

if a client with a sickness memory comes in with a cold, I am likely to spend several minutes discussing how the client is doing, whether there is someone to care for him, and the like. There should be tissues at the ready. In addition, it can be assumed that this issue is alive and fully operational outside the therapy office.

let's say you decide to work with Amazon tribes who have never been contacted by Westerners. Will their EMs be adequately described by your system?"

Expressed most broadly, I think memory types describe what a culture values or considers important. If mastery is deemed most important, then memories will disproportionately emphasize mastery experiences. Memory types, I think, will provide insight into what cultures value and emphasize. At Duke, where there was a high concentration of high achieving, competitive students, successful mastery memories were common in my research samples.

Section VII material broadly describes the cultural filter we use to filter and process perceptions. Will Section VII memory themes be found cross-culturally? I think several will hold up. For example, I think separation memories would show up almost universally in cultures where a primary mother-child relationship is encouraged. Also, mastery memories and injury, sickness, and hospitalization memories. But I predict we will also discover new content and process themes. Such as? I would be surprised if we did not find some non-Western groups who did not report "ancestor dream memories," which I would describe as dreams about relatives now in spirit. There may also be prophetic memories, and memories that reflect customs and practices not broadly accepted by mainstream Western cultures. A study of traditional Japanese, who tend to be Buddhist in their spirituality, might provide an interesting comparison group to Westerners. I encourage research to test the universality of Section VII material to see how cultural differences can affect the selection and organization of autobiographical material.

I view the taxonomic matters discussed in this chapter as turning a page into a new area of personal memories. Autobiographical memories help us understand how we as individuals see our world. A taxonomy of autobiographical memories will help us understand how the world can be seen, not just by Americans but by human beings however they are affected culturally.

11 It Is Impossible to Treat Criminals with Insight-Oriented Psychotherapy . . . True?

Most women in U.S. prisons were, first, victims.

More than 60% of incarcerated women report having been sexually assaulted before the age of eighteen.

Two-thirds of those working as prostitutes disclosed having been sexually abused as children—and more than 90% said they never told anyone. Only 1% reported having received counseling.

(S. Burton & C. Lynn, 2017, pp. v, 26, & 46)

If you believe that you have devised a powerful alternative to traditional insight-oriented psychotherapy, and you want to demonstrate efficacy, why not test it on the "untreatable"? One obvious choice would be a criminal population.

Raise the difficulty level. How about substance-abusing criminals? Neither population is treated impressively with insight-oriented therapy, correct?

Raise it again. How about criminals multiply incarcerated for substance-abuse-related crimes? That would be an operational definition of a career criminal with substance-abuse problems. Impossible, correct? In 1995 that was the consensus in the field, and it remains so today.

An esteemed colleague, Henry Richards, then affiliated with Friends' Research, approached me around the time I published the first non-edited book on early memories (Bruhn, 1990b) and the EMP (Bruhn, 1989a). Would I like to test memories work on multiply incarcerated women

Insight-Oriented Psychotherapy 83

convicted of substance-abuse-related crimes? And spend the next five years doing it in a prison? And undertake this treatment in groups, versus working with inmates individually? Why not? How many opportunities like this does one get in a lifetime? For me this would be like joining my boyhood heroes, Lewis and Clark, on an exploration of the unknown, then called the Northwest territories.

First question: How to rehabilitate inmates? Thousands of extremely talented therapists have tried insight-oriented therapy with prison inmates and failed. The bones of their failures litter prison yards across the country. No secret. If anything was impossible clinically, that was impossible.

Yet, incredibly, I believed I might be able to succeed. I had been working in my private practice with a subset of criminals and substance abusers who responded well to memories work. To be honest, I had no success with pedophiles. Domestic abusers? Some. Criminals not including pedophiles? That was not as hard. Substance abusers? Some success with outpatients but it was much easier once they had been abstinent a few months and stabilized.

I made a few preliminary observations. Criminals and substance abusers had often been traumatized. I was beginning to wonder whether criminality, at least in a large subset of criminals, might be a reaction to trauma. My thinking, from a criminal's perspective, went something like this: "If you treat me badly, why should I treat you any better?" A common human response. Perhaps traumatic experiences led to bonding problems and a deficit in empathy. An intriguing premise. It was an extremely long shot, but it was possible that a group treatment model focused on traumas might produce a more robust treatment result than open-ended, gradually unfolding individual insight-oriented psychotherapy. Why group? Inmates could see that others had suffered similar experiences—perhaps even worse. Support might develop. But it was a super long shot to premise that a failure of empathy to develop because of traumas might be the root cause of criminal behavior, at least in a large subgroup of criminals, and that memories work might provide the method needed to assess and heal individuals mired in a criminal lifestyle.

I had another huge advantage, however. Peter DeMuth and I (DeMuth & Bruhn, 1997) field-tested a preliminary memories work model with groups of substance-abusing offenders and had excellent results; I surmised the method might work as well or even better with a female population. Here is what DeMuth, the treating clinician and lead author, found:

> Use of the EMP enables individuals to get in touch with their own issues much more quickly than in traditional psychotherapy models, leaving more time for resolving the underlying issues that prompted the client to seek treatment. The written format of the EMP also

84   *Insight-Oriented Psychotherapy*

permits clients to access feelings, and sometimes previously suppressed memories as well, that might have consumed considerable one-on-one treatment time to uncover. The similarity of the maladaptive patterns evident in their memories with the same patterns acted out in present time provides a perspective for clients that is not easy to

unique experiences but are representative, instead, of the majority of inmates participating in the program.

(DeMuth & Bruhn, 1997, p. 33)

Because DeMuth was the sole clinician in the 1997 study, it should have been clear from the beginning of the Women's Prison Study that I brought no secret magic to group work since I never worked on the DeMuth treatment site. But the DeMuth and Bruhn (1997) study, for me, dropped the odds-on success to something closer to 3:1—still unlikely but deserving a speculative investment of five years on this ultrahigh-risk project.

Before I began group work the first day, my Friends' Research project colleagues warned me multiple times in the strongest possible terms: "Do not try to con cons. They are way better at it than you are. They will smell a con a million miles away. Be truthful. Be honest." Excellent advice for this novice part-time corrections psychologist. The smell of naivete must have been oozing from my pores.

And so, on a broiling hot day in 1995, I entered the women's prison to meet my first group.

"Everybody" told me memories work would fail. The prison administration dispatched a group of four professionals to the prison guardhouse on my first day to speed me back home and jettison the project. Their message was that many others before me had come through these gates intending to do good; all had failed. Their message was accurate and on point. Still, I had to try this.

Insight-Oriented Psychotherapy 85

I had set aside three months to design the approach, which was grounded on the EMP and an enhancement of the memories work module I reported in DeMuth and Bruhn (1997). We would share in a group of 10–12 inmates various kinds of memories as we journeyed incrementally into more challenging, traumatic memories. We would approach trauma not from an "I have been badly damaged" perspective but from a "What can I do about this?" perspective. In other words, the group would not just be about connecting with trauma and venting feelings, it would emphasize resolving the issues that emerged post trauma. Friends' allotted 20 three-hour once-a-week group sessions to complete these goals.

Anyone who has worked with prison inmates becomes quickly aware they operate from a foundation of power and control. They despise weakness and loathe having to share recollections that display personal vulnerabilities. For inmates, being vulnerable and unmasked in a predatory prison environment is an open invitation to be victimized again. Is it any wonder that insight-oriented therapy had been such a resounding failure?

I knew that memories work must circumvent similar therapeutic death traps. Even the slightest hint of "we are all human here, let's own our traumas" would stick a knife in the heart of the group.

"What if," I thought, "we adapted basic martial arts concepts to the problem? What if we went with the resistance? What would that look like?"

I was challenged in the first five minutes of Session 1: "We don't want to talk about our childhood traumas; living them once was enough." I told the inmate:

> You have a valid point. Memories work is about empowerment. We will develop skills that will make you stronger and more capable than you were before you began the group. You will know more, be able to do more, and handle more situations than you could before you came.

These were all seasoned criminals. To their ears, what I said was a con, and a rather weak con at that.

I had to win (or at least not lose) in the first five minutes, or the five-month memories group would have died there. Most inmates had already been exposed to insight-oriented therapy from well-intended and highly skilled professionals, and they knew from personal experience what I was selling. They loathed the product. I had to offer something that would benefit them and make them stronger. Did they believe what I told them? Absolutely not. They did not trust me and had no reason to. My initial goal was to establish credibility.

86 Insight-Oriented Psychotherapy

I offered a preliminary example. We began with an innocuous memory—not something traumatic. "What do memories tell us?" The inmates were hugely hesitant. Finally, an inmate offered a benign memory, like having a birthday party. My interpretation: "This is a positive affect memory. This is something you want—to be special. To be accepted. Valued. To

broken them down. Our primary goal was to empower them and make them stronger and more effective. Those negative memories not only told us what was wrong, if we put them together with their positive memories, they gave us some ideas about what needed fixing and how that might be done.

They weren't so sure about that. I asked for some mildly negative memories—not the traumatic ones. Someone volunteered an injury memory,[1] a common memory type in a clinical population (see Table 11.1). I said:

> Everyone has injury memories. We are vulnerable. We get hurt. When that happens, can we count on others to care about us enough to help? To take care of us? That memory reminds us of what we experienced—good or bad—and sets the table next time we get hurt or sick. Do I believe I will be helped? Let's see, what happened when . . . ?

More nods. I was getting through. More simple truths. I asked for more examples. Some memories were more troubling than others. I pointed out that memories might preserve the history, but they also help us connect with our expectations. I said, "There is nothing to fear about your expectations. Knowledge is power. Once you know, you can do something. Then you can have control."

I saw some nods. They were beginning to see what I was talking about. "Now," I said, "that gets us to traumatic memories.[2] Why do those

Insight-Oriented Psychotherapy 87

Table 11.1 Rank Order of 16 CEMSS-R Content and Process Themes in a Clinical Sample

Rank Order Content/Process Theme (Number)	Common Meaning (Percentage)
1 (1) Sickness, accidental injury, hospitalization	14.0 Can I depend on others to help me?
2 (11) Succorance	13.3 Trust
3 (5) Trust	12.7 Trust
4 (8) Successful mastery	10.7 Need achievement, self-confidence
5 (3) Separation, abandonment, being lost	10.0 Anxious attachment
6 (2) Losses	8.7 Bonding, grief
7 (4) Mastery failure	7.3 Lacks confidence
8 (13) Nonaggressive rule breaking	4.7 Integrity
9.5 (10) Being gifted/having picture taken	4.0 Feeling special
9.5 (12) Food	4.0 Possible eating disorder; neediness
11.5 (14) Aggressive/sexual impulse control	2.7 Impulse control
11.5 (16) Nothing scorable	2.7
13.5 (6) Rejection	2.0 Social issues, confidence
13.5 (9) Cooperative play	2.0 Connection, socializing
15 (7) Punishment	1.3 Social expectations, limits
16 (15) Bizarre material	0.0 Psychotic issues

The table is adapted from Bruhn (1995a).

Content and Process themes describe the most prominent needs and issues that appear in therapy cases. If a client offers six memories in Part I of the EMP describing trust issues, for example, the presenting problem likely will involve trust. In memories work with National Institute of Drug Abuse (NIDA) Women's Prison inmates, I identified the key issue in a memory and tried to resolve or mitigate it after considering the strongest needs in positive affect memories.

It should not be surprising that many clients new to therapy bring with them trust issues of the type: "Can I depend on others to help me?" Consider, for instance, the top three most common content and process themes. Memory content often hints at the degree of mistrust and reveals the issues likely to trigger this response, as discussed in Bruhn (1995b).

memories make us feel awful? What to do with them?" This conversation with my first group did not take place in Session 1. I introduced it around Session 3 or 4, when we had covered the basics of what memories are and how to interpret them. The inmates in following groups were on fire with memories they wanted to get out but only after word got around the prison from my first group that what I was doing actually helped. With this population especially, I tried to put everything on the table rather than tap dance difficult topics.

88   Insight-Oriented Psychotherapy

In the first few sessions my first group was predictably resistant. I was this crazy person who wanted to drag them bleeding through hell imbedded on their traumatic memories. I was this lunatic trying to con them to walk barefoot over a bed of hot coals and not only convince them this wouldn't hurt but make them believe this process would help them! I had

tion over and correct the misunderstanding. But nothing would calm the neighbor down. The stepfather walked away, and the neighbor attacked him from behind, stabbing him multiple times. He died on the balcony of their apartment as they waited for an ambulance. His dying words were, "I love you" and "Happy birthday." A footnote added to the pathos: His birthday was the same day as hers. He died on *their* birthday.

From that moment, her life changed irretrievably. Her mother had trouble with her because she reminded her so much of her late husband. And her mother expected her to take care of her siblings now that her father was dead—as we pieced it together, to assume his burden and his role. Alas, the family fell into poverty without a breadwinner available. The mother began to depend on drugs to escape from her problems.

As much as she loved her father before, my client began to hate him for having "left" her with this mess in her life. She hated her mother for treating her this way. And she developed a fantasy of finding the man who killed her father and avenging his death. She wrote threatening letters to him. In response, the man taunted her from his prison cell and invited her to do her worst.

As she got older, she became progressively depressed and involved with drugs, as her mother had. Her life centered around procuring drugs and getting high. She began to forget why she had started using in the first place. Over time, she was sent to prison on multiple occasions for charges related to her drug use, which occasioned her arrival in my memories group. What did she want from this group, I asked her? She wanted to excise this all-consuming, overpowering rage from within. Even in prison, the client was so rageful that she presented a general danger to anyone who might innocently set her off.

The key element in her treatment was grief work. I asked her to write and deliver a memorial speech, the sort of thing one might do at a funeral, to her stepfather, but a very personal one, and from the heart. She agreed to do so and took several weeks to prepare it. In her speech, she talked to her stepfather about her relationship to him, what that relationship meant, how things had changed as a result of his death, and that her only wish was to avenge his death. Aside from killing the perpetrator, she had no idea what to do with her life. Her speech was profound and moving. After her speech was finished, I requested that she ask her stepfather, who I reminded her was "seated" in the empty chair I had placed in front of her, what she should do. Crying throughout and in deep pain, she reported that he would tell her to let it go, that this man was not worth killing, that she should let the criminal justice system take care of it, and that he loved her, she was special to him, and she deserved better than the life she was now leading. This report was accompanied by a flood of tears and racking sobs that doubled her over.

At the end of the session, she stated that she felt much better. In subsequent weeks she reported that her homicidal fantasies were diminishing and that she was now focusing on how to put her ruined life back in order. I reminded her that she had children who needed her as much as she needed her father. This seemed to help her organize herself—along with my message that she had now learned to "talk" to her father, who would now be forever present for her whenever she needed him and was available for "advice" when she felt stuck.

I do not know what happened to her post group, but I can say this: [At the end of group] . . . I experienced her as one of the warmest, kindest, most compassionate people I have ever met, in prison or out. What made things change for her? I can't say for certain, but I think she learned how to reconnect with her father. Which made all the difference.

Word flew through the prison after this session that Bruhn could really help with traumas. I first learned about the sensation our group was causing when I was pulled aside by Henry Richards, who had told me little about my formal role in the study. Essentially, he said, memories work was designated to serve as the straw man condition, to be compared with the experimental treatment, Therapeutic Community, which had long been established as the only effective treatment for sociopathic

90 *Insight-Oriented Psychotherapy*

subjects. Nothing else was a close second. The NIDA study paradigm was as follows:

> Condition A (Therapeutic Community, Experimental Condition) was tested for efficacy against Condition B (Memories Work,

Richards told me. There had been a revolt in the Therapeutic Community study population. Once they learned what was happening in the memories work population, the Therapeutic Community group refused to continue unless they were guaranteed a memories work group treatment. This is the first time, as best as we could determine, a prison population ever revolted to *get* insight-oriented therapy. The original design of the NIDA study was ruined: $2.5 million on a five-year sponsored study down the drain. A midcourse change had to be made, Richards said, or the study was done. He asked my opinion.

Richards's premise had been that the Therapeutic Community group would move in a positive direction on indexed personality variables and that there would be signs of personal growth. But he could no longer precede thusly because the Therapeutic Community group demanded memories work in order to continue. I suggested that the outcome measure be switched to a recidivism statistic.

Adopting a recidivism measure was a huge gamble. Why? Making that change set a much higher bar than "positive changes on personality variables." Inmates could recidivate for relatively minor reasons, which frequently happened in the crucible of real life. Adopting an outcome measure like recidivism required belief and courage.

As a result of this discussion, the paradigm in the study was revised as follows:

> Condition A (Therapeutic Community, Experimental Condition) was tested for efficacy against Condition B (Memories Work, Treatment Control), and both were indexed against Condition C (No Treatment)

Insight-Oriented Psychotherapy 91

to determine whether recidivism statistics were impacted. Condition A now received both Therapeutic Community and Memories Work—a *double* treatment dose.

What were the results?

The study results demonstrated that recidivism in the treated population post release was reduced by 52%. There was no significant difference between the Therapeutic Community experimental group and the memories work treatment control group, not surprising when you consider many (nearly all) of the Therapeutic Community women also received memories work.

Richards concluded: "the pattern of incarceration, return to drug use, re-arrest and eventually return to prison through drug use can be broken through effective substance abuse treatment" (June 3, 1999 press release, Appendix B).

Did memories work outperform Therapeutic Community treatment? There was no data to support that premise. But consider that the difference in treatment time received by the two groups varied by more than 200:1.

Did Therapeutic Community outperform memories work? There is no data to support that premise either. What can we conclude? If the women received at least three months of treatment, their recidivism rate fell by 52% in relation to untreated controls. As Richards put it, "the longer women remained in treatment the lower their rate of re-arrest" (June 3, 1999 press release, Appendix B).

Briefly, rehabilitative treatment works, and the more help the women received in the study, the better the result in terms of recidivism. As also occurred with the DeMuth and Bruhn (1997) subjects, memories work was extremely well received by inmates. The present study adds heft to the earlier study results by demonstrating inmates were also able to remain out of prison after receiving treatment.

Memories work could reduce our prison population by an estimated 30%, based upon the large numbers of persons incarcerated for substance-abuse-related crimes. Memories work is not recommended to treat and release serial killers, murderers, or other violent offenders. But the study demonstrates that individuals multiply convicted of substance-abuse-related crimes (a very common class of crimes) can be treated effectively. A 52% reduction in recidivism is excellent. But until further research can be done, Therapeutic Community treatment is recommended in tandem with memories work because it is not known whether the two in combination interact to reduce recidivism by a greater percentage than either in isolation.

Where did memories work not have a beneficial effect? If an inmate reported a trauma or a loss, chances were we could find a way to mitigate the effects of the trauma. But when was memories work likely to fail? When the individual was organized like someone who attempts to have power and remain in control while not having empathy. The following is an example.

92 *Insight-Oriented Psychotherapy*

EM: This girl challenged me to a fight. A group of kids gathered around to watch. I hit her. Hard. She went down. I hit her again and again. I would have killed her if some kids had not pulled me off her. (Strongest feeling?) It felt good to hit her and hit her. I felt strong and completely in control. [Note: she was imprisoned for stabbing her

in return for a handshake and a signed certificate of completion, which often elicited a flood of proud tears. I personally signed and presented each certificate in front of the group. I tried to be generous in acknowledging publicly in front of her group what the inmate accomplished.

Initially, the prison administration labeled as me charismatic, and they suggested that no one else could have ever achieved these results.

I countered with a proposal: that the administration select two uncharismatic professionals by their criteria, and I would train them to do what I did. They accepted. The two new memory work therapists sat in on my groups for one 20-week rotation as "interns" before they were assigned their own groups. As novice memories work therapists, they produced recidivism results that were statistically equivalent to mine, which provided additional support for the efficacy of memories work. The present research strongly supports the premise that memories work as a method is teachable, especially when the results of DeMuth and Bruhn (1997) are taken into account.

I am sometimes asked to compare memories work and Therapeutic Community treatment for effectiveness. The Therapeutic Community model has a long history of demonstrated efficacy. Until the NIDA study Therapeutic Community remained the platinum standard treatment choice. Because of the study design, the fairest conclusion is that both methods are extremely effective. Unquestionably, memories work is far less expensive and time-consuming however.

During the study the U.S. Probation and Parole Office learned about the success of memories work with female inmates in the NIDA study.

Insight-Oriented Psychotherapy   93

They asked a group from the NIDA study to submit a grant proposal so they could refer a group of untreated (mostly male) violent offenders imminently due for release for anger management treatment and memories work in 12 sessions. Our proposal was immediately accepted. This work successfully continued through two grant cycles, and to the best of my knowledge once parolees started group and experienced a session or two, they finished (roughly 90% completion), and there was no recidivism during group. As was true with our female population, male parolees gave abundant evidence of trauma in their memories. Didactic material about anger was presented by my co-leader. Both aspects were seen as helpful by group members.

It has thus been demonstrated that inmates and parolees who complete a memories work module will show a substantial reduction in recidivism relative to untreated control subjects.

I should also disclose that I was also changed by offering memories work. Inmates appreciated memories work enormously, and their enthusiastic acceptance of what we were doing inspired me. This was one of the most positive clinical experiences of my professional life. No method will work 100% of the time with a large sample of inmates, but the reduction in recidivism from 60% to 28% over the criterion period with this population was close to miraculous.

Notes

1 Injury memories were the most prevalent among 16 categories of CEMSS-R (Last & Bruhn, 1991) content and process themes (Section VII). EMPs were obtained from patients from an outpatient mental health sample near the beginning of therapy. Bruhn (1995b) found that 14% of the sample were categorized as injury memories (see entire tabular results, Table 11.1). Knowing what the 16 categories were, and what they were likely to convey psychologically, provided an advantage in the Women's Prison study since it was not necessary to speculate about what the memory might mean. The meaning of "Injury," for instance, was well known and well described (Bruhn, 1995b).
2 My hypothesis—unstated to the groups—was that many inmates are incarcerated, indirectly, because of the effects of traumas they experienced. The affects that are triggered are medicated with alcohol and/or various drugs. Memories work helps inmates reorganize traumatic experiences so they can integrate what happened to them. Although the causes were various, many of the inmates were trapped in time warps by their traumas, which were reactivated in present time by psychologically similar triggers.

12 Conclusions

What Determines Whether an Experience is Retained in Long-Term Autobiographical Memory?

On what basis are experiences retained? The first sort emphasizes feelings. Extremity is key. Very unpleasant experiences are highlighted and spotlighted; these elements are to be avoided if possible. On the other hand, very pleasant experiences are marked to be repeated if possible.

Next, the mind organizes experiences by categories that approximate those evident in Section VII content and process themes. If the most negative experiences involve separations and abandonment, this category has priority. If being special is the most positive experience, then memories of being gifted may stand out; or perhaps being celebrated with a party. When a current experience highlights the satisfaction of a strong need, the likelihood of recall is also increased. Whether strongly positive or negative, the theme or need that is featured is likely retained as part of a set of similar experiences. If being abandoned by mother at home at age four is the featured memory, there are likely a set of memories with the same theme available for recall. Why is the featured memory chosen from the set? That memory best describes the individual elements of the theme that are troublesome for the individual. And thus it stands out from the rest. What elements? Mother may have promised not to leave and did; promised to read a story and didn't; promised not to drink and did, which is why she left; etc. Those will be triggering elements for experiences in present time.

When repetitive negative experiences are not resolved, their negativity increases with each failure. For instance, assume a repeating negative memory where the father gets drunk on Saturday night and pulls his child out of bed to beat him after he staggers home. If there is no way to mitigate the negativity of what occurs, the time before Saturday night becomes progressively more tense. Each additional beating adds depth and potential nuance to the trauma. What makes a situation like this so traumatic? Short of taking a huge risk, the victim has no control and no power to influence the outcome. Remembering such experiences reminds the individual about dangers he can't control and the paradoxical need to avoid the inevitable. This expectation creates tension. How are such problems resolved?

In Benjamin Franklin's "EMP," Franklin, who was indentured for seven years to his older brother to become a printer, was beaten regularly (Bruhn, 2006). Young Franklin endured the beatings while he continued to learn all he could to prepare himself for an independent life. However, the more he learned, the more unbearable was the brutality he experienced, and he decided to run away from Boston to Philadelphia where he established himself as a printer beyond—he hoped—the reach of his brother and the law. Sometimes geographical cures work if you are not arrested.

If individuals manage to free themselves from their psychological prison, then the negativity of, to pick an example, abandonment memories, decreases. They say, "I used to be very upset when I was left by myself, but I have worked that out. Now I watch a game with Joe, I meditate, I read a book, I play solitaire, or I go to a movie . . ." As abandonment becomes less painful, that issue is replaced by the next most toxic issue. How can what happens be described? The individual is no longer triggered as strongly by abandonment as in the past. Categories of memories appear to be stored on something analogous to a rotating wheel; place and priority are determined by how negative the affect is in the memory. In the case of very positive affect, an addiction needs to be ruled out. The degree of affective positivity or negativity commonly decreases as the problem is worked on, so intensity becomes an approximate quantitative signal of how severe the problem is.

If we don't attempt to alter the contextual expectations in a negative affect memory, the memory is likely to remain as previously recollected. The feelings will remain invariant. And individuals will be triggered now by the material that triggered them in the memory. Something must change for the memory to be processed differently. We must learn something we don't know, or we must acquire skills we did not have. If the person who triggers us does not change,

(continued)

96 Conclusions

(continued)

we must change—leave, acquire skills, or develop a more nuanced understanding that was lacking before. Else, the memory will continue to depict what was recalled previously—there is no reason for the memory to change.

work in the morning, we leave with an oft-remembered backpack of experiences that accompany us during the day. If nothing happens to change how we perceive these experiences, how we view things today will strongly resemble how we see things tomorrow. Time alone does not "cure."

What we do during that time will make all the difference. Which is what made memories work so impactful in the National Institute of Drug Abuse (NIDA) study. Many inmates used to tell me, "I don't feel like I am doing time any more. I feel like I am doing something with my time."

As we view the internal process from afar, perceptions make all the difference. In the end, despite the beatings and the trauma, the world we experience is our own invention. If it isn't working, we can fix it.

This book also highlights two major breakthroughs that emerged from 46 years of research and theoretical modeling with memories and their construction.

First Breakthrough

Bergson offered a wide-angle perspective on how memory operates through the principle of utility. Some memories are retained; others dropped. How does that happen? No one had been able to explain

Conclusions 97

how memories were selected for retention, organized, and clustered in groups (principle of attraction) for priority access and storage. Cognitive-Perceptual theory (Bruhn, 1985, 1990a, b) laid the foundation, but the present book clarifies how the process works by reverse-engineering various types of individual autobiographical memories to deduce and specify their structure and function. Through this process one can better understand how memories are programmed by analyzing the key elements used in their construction. This is the first time a metapsychological contextual theory (Cognitive-Perceptual) has been used (following Pepper, 1942) to explain how autobiographical memory works.

The elements the mind uses to program memories to become perceptographs are also identified. Psychic energy is used to make certain memories stand out for attention via clarity. Affect (positive and negative) is used to identify a memory as reflecting needs (positive affect) in deficit or as highlighting issues (negative affect) that require resolution. Memory events that are recurring in an EMP (such as punishment) further emphasize important issues (negative affect) or strong needs (positive affect). Recurring process and content themes (CEMSS-R, Section VII) across different memories provide emphasis and increase our confidence of importance as well as providing nuance and specificity. Spontaneous, versus directed, memories tell us that the underlying content or process theme is significant to the client, as opposed to the person requesting the memory (e.g., first school memory, a directed memory). And so, the mind uses various aspects or elements in memories to emphasize importance, convey meaning, and to direct the reader to the imbedded message.

Second Breakthrough

The second breakthrough challenges a long-held axiom in clinical psychology that insight-oriented psychotherapy, specifically memories work as reported here and in DeMuth and Bruhn (1997), cannot be effectively used to work with traumas and rehabilitate criminals. It has long been believed criminals are far too impulsive and insufficiently introspective and reflective to profit from insight-oriented psychotherapy. I used to wonder whether insight-oriented therapy was inherently flawed or whether the technique was being misapplied to this population. My surmise: The failure rested mainly in the nature of the technique. How so?

A classic insight-oriented approach leaves the inmate, by self-report, feeling more vulnerable and more damaged than before treatment. What memories work—also insight oriented—does that differs from gradually unfolding insight-oriented psychotherapy is that it empowers inmates and increases their functionality, which draws them to the process. The NIDA study clarifies and extends the findings of DeMuth and Bruhn (1997), who reported that inmates accepted memories work because the process helped them work through and resolve their traumas. It thus empowered

98 *Conclusions*

them, rather than leaving them feeling weak and more vulnerable, as had been true with traditional insight-oriented psychotherapy. The NIDA replication study extends DeMuth and Bruhn by demonstrating that memories work contributed to a 52% reduction of recidivism over the criterion period, and it did so with over 99% less professional time than

also demonstrated in the study that other therapists could be trained to provide memories work with no significant reduction in recidivism.

Closing Thoughts

We have advanced our knowledge considerably in the last 46 years about the selection and retention of autobiographical memories: How positive and negative affect memories work in concert to suggest how issues can be resolved; how to identify in about a minute the issues in a critical memory that motivate a client to seek help; and how to use load-bearing memories to resolve presenting problems in therapy. An effective use of memories also builds trust: Clients know the therapist understands their problems when the memory itself becomes a focus of treatment. Therapist and client both understand that the memory is not just an historic event that happened long ago—it is as alive today in the present moment as it ever was.

Excessive stress, which impacts the mind–body link tied to the immune system, can precipitate the development of many diseases. The source of the stress is most often evident via anxiety and anger in an EMP protocol. My patient with end-stage sarcoidosis responded so well to memories work that her disease process was disrupted, her immune system reasserted itself, and she was "cured." I think we will find that memories work lowers the level of background stress that may compromise the immune system from warding off disease. I have experienced similar results with many patients who have other "psychosomatic" illnesses, the course of which is also believed to be highly impacted by stress-related variables.

Unlike many insight-oriented therapies, memories work is relatively straightforward to learn. I can teach a graduate student how to identify the memory most closely involved with a client's request for psychotherapy in about a minute from the EMP. The memories work involved to resolve it may be more complex. In Fred's case (see Chapter 9, Example 2), however, I simply redirected his attention to what he was not seeing— what others who knew him best respected the most. In other cases, a series of interacting structures evident in memories need to be taken down and replacements constructed. In each case the guiding question is: What is not working here, and what needs to be modified? For instance, the prison inmate who lost her father needed to find out how to reconnect with him.

In 1899 Freud published what was to become a foundational text in clinical psychology with his classic, *The Interpretation of Dreams*. This powerful book proposed dreams as the royal road to the unconscious, and analysis as the way to help patients recover their repressed memories. Does analysis work? Yes. It can indeed help recover repressed memories. It can also help us understand what may have caused us to suffer damage and experience limitations from our childhood.

The EMP offers an alternative to the psychoanalytic method of recovering memories.

The central question from my perspective is this: What do we aspire to do as clinicians? Recover repressed memories and free up the energy thus committed to keeping them repressed? Or are we interested in discovering what brings clients in for therapy and helping them work through the issues identified in their EMPs? Memories work and the EMP offer an alternative approach to traditional insight-oriented therapy as we reconceptualize what we can offer clients.

Does memories work as an insight-oriented therapy offer anything unique?

The NIDA study results speak for themselves. When a prison revolt occurs so inmates can obtain memories work, that by itself speaks to efficacy. The 52% reduction in recidivism adds an exclamation mark. What made memories work so effective with this population? More research is needed, but from my own experience as a group leader, I suspect that we will find memories work is incredibly effective with trauma victims, whether they be incarcerated in prisons, or damaged by war experiences, or compromised by molestations. I think we will also find that in cases of trauma, group therapy with similarly situated persons will be more effective than individual therapy because support will come from other participants who truly understand and care and are willing to support other group members emotionally.

Epilogue

This is a foundational book about personality assessment and what happens when the mind, life experiences, and autobiographical memory come together to produce successive iterations of personality. If asked at various ages to produce the equivalent of an EMP, most of us could

ing foundational memory concepts: "Recollections merely reflect . . . the person's perceptual framework within which he interpret[s] life's experience" (p. 302). If we want to reduce the role of memories to one sentence, it is hard to improve upon Mosak, whose thinking about assessment work with memories provided a helpful reality check for me as a young graduate student.

To which I would add: "Perceptual frameworks," thankfully, can change over time. How we understand the world at age 20 is probably not the way it will be understood at age 50 if we remain open to new ideas.

George Eliot put her own spin on the idea of change, which is foundational to memories work: "It is never too late to become what you might have been." How could this be said any better? Change is always possible.

Case Study

Harry (composite identity) was a 45-year-old divorced man recently released from jail for various substance-abuse-related offenses. Like many ex-offenders, he struggled to obtain employment after his release from prison, partly because he could not pass a drug-alcohol screen. He lived on social security disability in a group home until he finished parole and could find employment. He stated that he could not maintain sobriety because of his compulsion to drink. He felt he should be able to stop because he stopped for over a year in jail, but he said he needed medication to help him get over his cravings. Benzos worked great, he said, but no psychiatrist would prescribe them because of a past history of abusing them.

My initial question was to assess whether something psychological might be driving his compulsion to drink. His history suggested many candidates, including a number of disappointments like his divorce, his estrangement from his children, failed relationships, and his trouble securing employment. Further back in his past there was also a career-ending knee injury as a high school senior that ended a promising sprinting career. How to determine what was might be the major driver of his cravings to drink?

I began with his EMP material.

The critical incident in his adult life from his EMP was as follows: He discovered his wife, whom he loved deeply, had had an affair with his best friend. He got drunk, jumped into his new sports car, and crashed it into a tree. After a cab brought him to work the next day, a fellow employee reported him to the police after over-hearing his story. He lost his license to drive and eventually his professional license. His wife divorced him, and the costs were astronomical, in part because he was found legally responsible for the divorce due to alcoholism. Partly because of inadequate legal representation, the state incarcerated him for a DUI. While incarcerated, he lost everything after extensive legal costs related to the divorce and inadequate attempts by his attorney to defend his license. During the subsequent legal hearings, he was required to pay child support and alimony to his ex-wife based on his past income history, not the $2,000/month SSI he was slated to receive. Of all these things, the worst

102 *Case Study*

for him was losing visitation with his children because, according to the court, his drinking presented a potential danger to his children.

When I began working with him—roughly seven years after the affair—he had been drinking whenever he could, a couple of bottles of wine or more per day. Over a five-year period he had been treated,

The *critical* problem emerged in a session as we worked on a key memory, the first in his EMP. He described a telephone conversation the previous night with his father, a lifelong teetotaler. He finally confronted him during this call with my encouragement. He wanted to come home to see his mother, who was ill. His father was hesitant. He noted every time he came home previously there was an emotional storm, which upset him. He said he would leave after each visit with the family in turmoil. His father said he did not want any more of that.

His comment prompted him to find his voice. He recreated the phone conversation with me in session.

> (Referring to Memory 1 in the EMP): [client to his father] "When I was four years old you pulled off your belt and beat me (rage in his voice)—how could you have beaten me?"
>
> What does this critical memory tell us?
>
> (Bruhn to client): "You are exploring the foundations of your relationship with your father: 'You are my father: HOW could you have beaten me? I was four years old! What did I *do* to justify that?'"
>
> Bruhn: "The answer is NOTHING. You are off the hook."
>
> Bruhn (continuing): "So you are saying the problem is on you (father). What is *his* problem?"
>
> Bruhn (continuing): "Your father's problem is not feeling in control, a feeling that disorganizes him."
>
> "But that doesn't make sense exactly. What did YOU do?"
>
> "Nothing."
>
> "Ok, Bruhn, so what was going on?" [I say to him rhetorically]

"He was beating HIS FATHER!"

"*What?*"

"His *father*."

"That doesn't make sense!"

"*His* father was a drunk. An alcoholic. He probably did many things that left your father as a child feeling angry and not in control. And crazy with anxiety and fear as a result.

So when YOU did things that left him feeling NOT in control, he flashed back to his file of memories with his father when he also felt not in control.

He could do nothing about that as a child. After all, he was a child. He was defenseless. All he could do then was survive.

But with you he was a *man*. As a man, he could stand up and defend himself.

So he pulled off his belt and beat you."

Obviously I was not speaking a literal, historical truth. I was reporting a probable emotional and psychological truth, and both follow their own rules of logic. To summarize the rest:

Ok, you (Harry) say, "So what? What's the next step?"

Answer: "You now know *the Truth*. You did nothing but trigger your father and remind him of his own traumas. That was your 'sin' [which obviously is not a sin]. I would say that was your 'calling'—to be a Truth teller. So now he had a chance to observe himself, recoil from his actions, and change.

He missed an opportunity."

"And now?"

"Pray for your father. You did nothing wrong. You were four years old. HE needs to heal. He needs to talk with someone.

And you?

There IS hope. But each of us must be tested and learn to repudiate violence as a way of handling problems in relationships and in acting out our feelings.

Even though you did not deserve to be whipped, you were whipped. Here's where you are stuck: 'What did I do?' Part of you wants to be responsible so you can change and not see the problem repeated."

The answer: "Nothing. You did not deserve the beating. You need to tell your father that now, simply and directly. Then pray for him and move on. Your ex-wife did not learn this lesson either. When you find the right person for you, you will find the right question to ask. Perhaps it is: 'When you have had problems with previous partners, how were these resolved?' Or: 'When did you become the angriest with a partner, and how did you deal with those feelings?'

Questions like these."

104   *Case Study*

Trust develops through experience. Memories can provide an idea of what a potential partner has learned in her life journey.

Now for the tougher question: What did this intervention do for Harry? It reframed how he saw himself. Before, he was the victim of powerful men, and he was abused. Now? He was someone who was

But his grandmother died. A replacement was needed. He now had a voice to keep his father at bay, but he had no grandmother who believed in him. He was alone. Vulnerable—as his memory of his brawl with his ex-wife demonstrated. Legally and emotionally vulnerable. And he felt betrayed on so many levels.

He needed someone to substitute for his grandmother. In the absence of any volunteers, his therapist needed to pinch hit. I did what I could. That opened an alternative path.

An alternative path where he was guided by what his grandmother had said about him. Only after he had rejected the negative treatment from his father and accepted the positive, could he begin to give up alcohol, which he had used to medicate his pain, anxiety, and emptiness. Before, he felt he was the antithesis of special—worthless and deserving of nothing. And so he drank.

One technique used in our work was to bring his grandmother back to life when he got stuck in a problem. His relationship with her was deep enough that he could immediately imagine what she might say to him in various circumstances. So I would invite grandmother to the session and ask her to provide her advice and perspective. Harry would do both voices in an animated, Oscar-worthy back and forth performance. At the end of each session with grandmother I noted the obvious: Grandmother had not died; she lived within him as always, available for a relationship, encouragement, and support. Each session helped to move us along incrementally as we refined the relationship, much as Milton Erickson did in his February Man case, discussed earlier in Chapter 9 (Example 8), only Harry played both roles.

Harry had a nested set of load-bearing memories (in contrast to the woman in Chapter 4 who was traumatized by the family guard dogs) that had to be successively reconfigured for him to give up alcohol and continue with his life. Harry's was a complex case involving painful, demeaning punishment by his father and a resulting mistrust that was exacerbated and amplified by his wife's affair with his best friend, the loss of his career and his children.

To provide a more realistic context, Harry's EMP memories of completing an accelerated training program in three years gave me a place to start. I told Harry, much as his grandmother might have, "I believe in you. *You have already climbed Mt. Everest.*" Previous life achievements that were challenging can often be used as if they were stepping stones to provide an alternative template for problems currently in process. In the mind, time does not exist—there are only a series of problems that need solutions. If he overcame "X" before, he can overcome "Y" now.

There was another angle to reducing Harry's compulsion to drink. Harry requested benzos, but these were likely to create another dependency. I consulted with colleagues for options, and the one that turned out to be most successful was a hemp-oil-based bottle of drops designed to treat anxiety issues. Harry was my first client to use this. There were no side effects in his case and no dependency issues. One of my colleagues told me it was her experience that hemp-oil drops could take a level 10 anxiety episode to a 2 or 3 at times. If Harry's case is at all representative, we may be learning more about hemp-oil drops in reducing anxiety in substance-abuse cases.

Two years into our work, Harry had successfully completed a lengthy probation; he was working out three times a week; he had successfully completed a month long alcohol research treatment program; he had tried several part-time working experiences; he had been sober for periods of 30 days or more; he had moved from a group home to an independent apartment; and he was starting to date occasionally. He was doing much better. Ideally, I would have preferred to work with Harry in a memories work group of ten individuals (see Chapter 11), but I could not find any other similarly situated clients and had to do individual work.

With its substance abuse, physical abuse, and profound history of loss, treatment in this case was enormously challenging and complex. But as we progressed, I viewed the struggle in this work as a competition between hate (when he was belted by father) and love (he was very bonded to his grandmother, who loved him unconditionally), with the goal of rebuilding trust. My role? To offer a voice to repudiate the beatings and the betrayal from his wife. To unconditionally repudiate the refusal of the system to so much as allow contact with his children, even with professional supervised visitation. I could then say something like this: "How you were treated was wrong. Period. But now we must address your substance abuse, or even more wrong things will happen, and neither of us will be able do anything about that. How can we make that happen?"

106 *Case Study*

Despite our work, he continued to struggle with alcohol, as in, two days sober, two days drunk; one week sober, three days drunk; and so forth. But the periods of sobriety incrementally lengthened. As these periods stretched, I noted how his mental acuity was returning, his strength and mental toughness improving, etc. I asked him if he was seeing what

less challenging.

Below I summarize assessment and treatment, stepwise in detail, to provide a more complete example of how memories can be utilized in the treatment of complex cases.

Using traditional psychiatric diagnostic criteria, how would this patient be diagnosed? As I see it now, bipolar 2 and some variation of chronic alcoholism along with mild borderline personality disorder. Using his autobiographical memories, I would also see him as having a previously undiagnosed case of PTSD associated with the belting by his father. As with many returning vets with PTSD, there was danger everywhere after he discovered his wife's affair, and he could count on no one for compassion with his grandmother deceased. In sum: he had a major untreated anxiety disorder and PTSD, which could have been diagnosed through EMP responses (Memory 1). What did he most need? Caring and compassion. And emotional support.

Harry is doing a lot better. There are zigs and zags. He drops in as needed.

Stepwise Use of the EMP to Find Where Client Is Stuck and What to Do

Presenting picture: Anxious and depressed after several incarcerations for multiple DUI/DWIs and having been de-licensed from driving and from practicing his profession. Barred from visiting his children. Daily alcohol use which re-commenced two months after more than a year's sobriety in jail.

Case Study   107

Clearest/most negative EM from Part 1, EMP: Memory 1. "My father was furious with me. He ripped off his wide leather belt. His face was a mask of hate. 'I'll teach you, you little shit!' He hit me again and again with his belt. Finally, he stopped, tired. I said, very upset: 'What did I do? What did I do?' He said nothing. He walked away to the kitchen. I could hear my grandma in the kitchen telling my mother (her daughter), 'You're not a good mother' [for letting my father beat me]. I was barely four years old."

Clearest Part: Being hit again and again with his belt.
Strongest feeling: Helpless, hopeless. "There was nothing I could do."
Clarity rating: 5 (extremely clear).
Affect rating: 1 (very negative).

Clearest/most positive memory from Part I (or, if none, the happiest memory in Part II): Memory 5. "I got all As on my report card. My grandma was so happy. She told me I was the smartest boy, and when I grew up I was destined to be extremely successful. She was the only person in my family like that with me. She loved me so much!"

---

1   Find most negative EM on the EMP: **Memory 1** (rated 1) on pp. 9–10.
2   Find clearest/most negative EM: **Memory 1** (5 clarity, 1 negative affect).
3   Précis of Memory 1: When those I am close to get angry with me, I expect brutal treatment (a beating or the equivalent) and rejection, and a refusal to talk through what made them angry. **Note:** An airing of grievances, discussion, and resolution of conflicts is impossible. **Content theme:** This is a punishment memory—subtype excessive punishment for something not done (see Bruhn & Schiffman, 1982b). See also Table 11.1 in this book—category 15. Memories of this type reduce to an expectation of a need for power and control from significant others—'you do what I tell you to do, and shut up.' How to weaken expectations like this? Encourage client to experience relationships where love and compassion predominate.
4   (Crosscheck) Is this memory the most important memory in Part I (see p. 11). If not, which is? (Review that memory, especially if affect is very negative.) [Memory 1 was in fact most important.]
5   Which is the clearest/most positive memory? Memory 5 (5 clarity, 7 positive affect), getting all As, which is appreciated by Grandma.
6   Strongest needs in Memory 5: Love in abundance, respect linked to achievement. Therapist occupies this role until others among client's relationships begin to manifest these qualities.
7   How most negative and most positive memories fit together: "I need to feel very successful and valued to counteract feelings of rejection associated with being beaten." Memories 1 and 5 in combination suggest splitting and borderline personality disorder.

(continued)

(continued)

8 Where I am stuck in my life: "I don't understand what makes men so angry at me. I can't get them to talk with me."

9 Bruhn: Call your father: Key question: "What did I do as a four-year-old to make you so angry as to beat me like that?"

relationship between cause and effect). Memory 5: Successful mastery (all As), with love and respect from Grandma resulting.

15 Integrating Memories 1 and 5: "I can gain acceptance and respect from being competent and successful while I try to learn how to talk with men and resolve conflicts with them."

16 Two key perceptographs are evident: "First, when I am rejected, I don't understand what caused the bad outcome. Second, when I achieve at a high level, those I love and trust appreciate and celebrate my accomplishments."

17 What happens at the intersection of these perceptographs? Anxiety when he feels rejected and is not achieving at a high level. Alcohol is used to medicate the anxiety that arises.

18 One key pivot in therapy: I asked him to invent a method to demonstrate sobriety by blowing into a breathalyzer and taking a photo that could be stored on the cloud. He would demonstrate sobriety 30 days consecutively. He did.

19 Second key pivot: I invited Grandma (now deceased) to take a chair in therapy and for the client to talk to her about his alcohol abuse. She told him he was her favorite and her special child and he was amazingly brilliant, but that alcohol made him "stupid." Grandma's favorite did NOT want to be "stupid." He committed to sobriety despite slips.

20 Third key pivot: He sent seasonal gifts to his children, who were cut off from him. He got a response from a daughter who told him that it was painful for her to maintain contact if he continued drinking. His interpretation: Once again, he had been rejected. I told him: "You now have a choice—your kids or alcohol. Which is more important to you?"

21 Breakthrough: He realized his contribution to losing visitation was developing a reliance on alcohol to cope with his feelings. He said he had always been an overachiever. He was the primary financial support of the family and hyper-responsible. He also knew he must stop drinking. For himself and to repair his relationship with his children.

22 Next breakthrough: Completely distraught. Confessed he loved his wife. He found her very attractive. He confessed he missed her terribly, which partly explained what drove him to drink excessively—heartbreak and loneliness. I noted that this phase of his life was over—she had remarried—but he had kept himself in good shape by working out. There would be the possibility for other substantial relationships when he stopped drinking.

23 In rehab after a slip, he met several friends, good people, who were closer to his level of functioning. Although they were good people, he could see that the work we had been doing put him at a much higher level of functioning. He left rehab grateful for these experiences, determined to beat his addiction.

24 A visit by his parents and older sister went beautifully. They saw him at his new apartment. No fights. Father shook his hand and wished him well. Mother was tearful and emotional. Visit was about as good as it gets emotionally. This was the first face-to-face contact in some time. Therapy continues, with significant improvement observed. When we began our work: Daily drinking, no friends, no life goals, high level of depression, high risk of incarceration for violation of parole. Presently: Longer periods of sobriety, lower level of depression, several friends, odd jobs, and an emotional reconnection with family. Work continues.

Appendix A
Content and Process Themes, CEMSS-R

subject)

a) Sickness
b) Hospitalization
c) *Accidental* injury

If a), b), or c) is checked, check one of the following if they apply:

i) Threat or damage is minimized.
ii) Threat or damage is maximized (e.g., emphasizes amount of blood, pain, fear, damage, or potential seriousness).

NOTE: If subject is *intentionally* hurt/injured, score "5d."
If injury is the result of *mastery failure*, consider "4a."
If injury is the result of *punishment*, consider "7."

2 **Losses**

a) A death occurs (person or pet; not other animals).
b) The family moves (others are left behind).
c) Someone leaves the family (e.g., parents separate, older sib goes away to college).
d) A significant other (parent, relative, friend, pet) is sick or accidentally injured. Or a pet is lost.

NOTE: DO NOT score "2" if a significant other or pet is intentionally hurt or killed by the subject; instead, consider "14a."

DO NOT score "2" if a significant other or pet is intentionally hurt or killed by another person; instead consider "5e."

3   **Separation, abandonment, or being lost**

    a) Accidental separation or being lost: An accidental or unintentional separation occurs, usually with the result that distress occurs (e.g., anxiety, fear, panic, insecure feelings).

    b) Intentional separation occurs although the caretaker may not intend harm (e.g., mother leaves child with baby sitter; mother goes to hospital to have baby; subject goes to school for first time).

4   **Mastery failure**

    a) Subject tries to achieve a goal and fails. This commonly involves a beginning, a process of learning, and an end (e.g., tries to learn how to ride bike and falls off; fails a math test).

    b) Someone else tries to achieve a goal and fails.

5   **Trust**

    a) A significant other is drunk.

    b) The subject is *sexually abused* (Score if process is exploitative, whether or not intercourse occurs).

    c) The subject is *neglected* (e.g., left outside in the rain or cold so the person feels unprotected).

    d) The subject is *physically* attacked; abused and deliberately harmed; or *threatened* with attack or abuse. (Attacker may be a person or animal.)

    e) Same as d) except the victim is another person or a pet.

NOTE: If the subject initiates or willingly participates in sexual contact with another child of a similar age, score "14b."

If the subject physically attacks another person, consider "14a."

6   **Rejection**

    a) The subject experiences social rejection from peers (e.g. peers would not play with her).

    b) The subject experiences verbal abuse from an authority figure (e.g. "you stupid . . . ")

7   **Punishment**

    a) The subject is punished for something for which he accepts responsibility. He does not believe the punishment to be excessive.

    b) Same as a), except the punishment is seen as excessive.

    c) The subject does not know why he is being punished or the subject is punished for something he states he did not do. The fairness of the punishment is therefore a material issue.

NOTE:

If punishment follows rule-breaking behavior, consider "13."

If punishment follows aggressive/sexual behavior, consider "14."

If punishment follows an unsuccessful mastery attempt, also consider "4a."

(continued)

(continued)

B   What appear to be Positive Affect EMs

  8   **Successful mastery**

    a)   The subject is involved in purposeful, constructive, goal-

NOTE: DO NOT score "9" if play is with adults, consider "11."

  10   **Being gifted or having a picture taken**

    a)   The focus is on receiving a gift, usually on a holiday or a birthday.
    b)   The emphasis is on having one's picture taken, either with the family or by oneself. (Typically, the affect is pleasure or excitement.)

  11   **Succorance**

    The focus is on being helped, cared for, or treated kindly, typically by a significant other or an authority figure (e.g., being rocked to sleep; being sung to; or being read a story).

NOTE:
If succorance follows mastery activity, consider "4" and "8."
If succorance follows accidental injury, consider "1e."
If succorance follows intentional injury/abuse of the subject, also consider "5."

C   PROCESS THEMES

  Memory may be positive, negative, or neutral in affect

  12   **Food**

    The focus is on food and eating (e.g., the subject is eating, looks forward to eating).

13 **Nonaggressive rule-breaking**

a) The subject does not respect socially appropriate rules or limits (e.g., lies, cheats, steals).

b) The subject does not respect appropriate rules or sanctions from authority (e.g., cuts school, disrupts classroom, defies parents, smokes, drinks alcohol, uses drugs).

If a) or b) is checked, check one of the following:

i) The rule-breaking is minor.

ii) The rule-breaking is moderate.

iii) The rule-breaking is serious (e.g., in terms of consequences, or potential consequences, of the subject's actions).

NOTE: If rule-breaking is aggressive, score "14a."
If rule-breaking is followed by punishment, and the focus (clearest part of memory) is on punishment, consider "7."

14 **Aggressive/sexual impulse control**

a) The subject is aggressive (e.g., is verbally abusive, hits others, pushes, sets a fire, attacks someone, breaks something, hurts an animal, or threatens to hurt a person or animal).

b) The subject initiates or participates willingly in a sexual activity with another child of similar age.

c) The subject is not in control of his physical self (e.g., runs into wall, tree).

NOTE: If the subject is sexually exploited/ sexually abused by someone else, score "5b."
If aggressive/sexual behavior is followed by punishment, and the focus (clearest part of memory) is on punishment, consider "7."

If a) is checked, check **one** of the following:

i) The aggression or threat is *minor* (e.g., pushes someone, curses at someone).

ii) The aggression or threat is *moderate* (e.g., gets in a scuffle, hits someone).

iii) The aggression or threat is *serious* (e.g., gets into a serious fight or brawl; attacks someone with a weapon; notes that control was lost; or sets a fire, even a small fire).

If b) is checked, check **one** of the following:

i) Curiosity appears to be the motivation (e.g., looking, touching).

ii) The subject is aroused and excited (e.g., fondling; may note that this was the first in a series of similar activities).

(continued)

(continued)

D   Memory cannot be scored

  15 **Bizarre material** The memory appears to reflect a psychotic or
      delusional process or the content of the memory is bizarre (e.g., a

Appendix B[1]
Press Release of NIDA Study Results

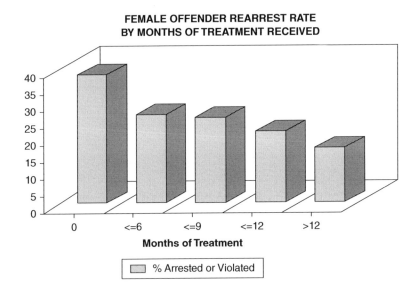

FOR IMMEDIATE RELEASE

MORE TREATMENT, FEWER REARRESTS FOR FEMALE OFFENDERS

Drug Program Offers Hope for Women Returning to Their Families

Jessup, Maryland — June 3, 1999 — Women with substance abuse problems frequently fail on probation or parole, primarily due to relapse to drug use. Preliminary data from a 5-year National Institute for Drug Abuse (NIDA) funded study in Maryland indicates that the pattern of incarceration, return to drug use, rearrest and eventually return to prison can be broken through effective substance abuse treatment.

The preliminary study compared outcomes for 72 women who did not receive treatment for their substance abuse problems with 94 women who

116 *Appendix B*

participated for at least three months in intensive treatment with professional therapists behind prison walls. Almost 60% of women with untreated substance abuse problems were rearrested on new charges or returned for violation of a conditional release within the 15 month follow-up period release, whereas the failure rate of women who received at least 3 months

References

Achenbach, T. M. (1991). *Manual for the Child Behavior Checklist/4–18 and 1991 Profile*. Burlington, VT: University of Vermont Department of Psychiatry.

Acklin, M. W., Bibb, J. L., Boyer, P., & Jain, V. (1991). Early memories as expression of relationship paradigms: A preliminary investigation. *Journal of Personality Assessment, 57,* 177–192.

Acklin, M. W., Sauer, A., Alexander, G., & Dugoni, B. (1989). Predicting depression using earliest childhood memories. *Journal of Personality Assessment, 53,* 51–59.

Adler, A. (1912/1917). *The neurotic constitution.* New York: Moffat, Yard.

Adler, A. (1927). *Understanding human nature.* New York: Greenberg.

Adler, A. (1929). *The case of Miss R: The interpretation of a life story.* New York: Greenberg.

Adler, A. (1931). *What life should mean to you.* New York: Grosset & Dunlap.

Adler, A. (1937). The significance of early recollections. *International Journal of Individual Psychology, 3,* 283–287.

Ansbacher, H., & Ansbacher, R. (Eds). (1956). *The individual psychology of Alfred Adler.* New York: Basic Books.

Bartlett, F. C. (1932). *Remembering: A study in experimental and social psychology.* Cambridge: Cambridge University Press.

Bergson, H. (1912/2004). *Matter and memory* (N. M. Paul & W. S. Palmer, Trans.). Mineola, NY: Dover Publications.

Binder, J. L., & Smokler, I. (1982). Early memories: A technical aid to focusing in time-limited dynamic psychotherapy. *Psychotherapy: Theory, Research and Practice, 17,* 52–62.

Bruhn, A. R. (1974). *Prediction of locus of control stance from the earliest childhood memory* (Unpublished major area research paper). Duke University, Durham, NC.

Bruhn, A. R. (1976). *Earliest memories of being punished as predictors of control stance* (Unpublished doctoral dissertation). Duke University, Durham, NC.

Bruhn, A. R. (1981). Children's earliest memories: Their use in clinical practice. *Journal of Personality Assessment, 45,* 258–262.

Bruhn, A. R. (1984). The use of early memories as a projective technique. In P. McReynolds & C. J. Chelume (Eds.), *Advances in psychological assessment* (Vol. 6, pp. 109–150). San Francisco, CA: Jossey-Bass.

118 *References*

Bruhn, A. R. (1985). Using early memories as a projective technique: The Cognitive-Perceptual method. *Journal of Personality Assessment, 49*, 587–597.

Bruhn, A. R. (1989a). *The early memories procedure.* Bethesda, MD: Author. (Available at www.arbruhn.com/store/).

Bruhn, A. R. (1989b). *The romantic relationships procedure.* Bethesda, MD: Author. (Available at www.arbruhn.com/store/).

www.arbruhn.com/store/).

Bruhn, A. R. (1995a). Early memories in personality assessment. In J. N. Butcher (Ed.), *Clinical personality assessment: Practical approaches* (pp. 278–301). New York: Oxford University Press.

Bruhn, A. R. (1995b). Ideographic aspects of injury memories: Applying contextual theory to the Comprehensive Early Memories Scoring System—Revised. *Journal of Personality Assessment, 65*, 195–236.

Bruhn, A. R. (2006). In celebration of his 300th birthday: Benjamin Franklin's Early Memories Procedure. *E-Journal of Applied Psychology, 2*(1), 22–44.

Bruhn, A. R. (2008). What makes EMDR work? [Review of the book L. Parnell *A Therapist's Guide to EMDR: Tools and Techniques for Successful Treatment*]. *PsycCRITIQUES, 53*, Release 30, Article 1554–0138.

Bruhn, A. R. (2015). The Early Memories Procedure and its origins. In R. Davido (Ed.), *Creative minds and methods in assessment psychology* (pp. 5–55). Scottsdale, AZ: Inkwell Productions.

Bruhn, A. R. (in press). A proposed integration of assessment and psychotherapy through memory work. *E-Journal of Applied Psychology.*

Bruhn, A. R. (forthcoming). *Can we treat the untreatable? Memories from hell.* Manuscript in preparation.

Bruhn, A. R., & Bellow, S. (1984). Warrior, general and president: Dwight David Eisenhower and his earliest recollections. *Journal of Personality Assessment, 48*, 371–377.

Bruhn, A. R., & Bellow, S. (1987). The Cognitive-Perceptual approach to the interpretation of early memories: The earliest memories of Golda Meier. In C. D. Spielberger & J. N. Butcher (Eds.), *Advances in personality assessment* (Vol. 6, pp. 69–87). Hillsdale, NJ: Erlbaum.

References   119

Bruhn, A. R., & Davidow, S. (1983). Earliest memories and the dynamics of delinquency. *Journal of Personality Assessment, 47*, 476–482.

Bruhn, A. R., & Feigenbaum, K. (forthcoming). *The interpretation of autobiographical memories*. Manuscript in preparation.

Bruhn, A. R., & Last, J. (1982). Early memories: Four theoretical perspectives. *Journal of Personality Assessment, 46*, 119–127.

Bruhn, A. R., and Schiffman, H. (1982a). Invalid assumptions and methodological difficulties in early memory research. *Journal of Personality Assessment, 46*, 265–267.

Bruhn, A. R., & Schiffman, H. (1982b). Prediction of locus of control stance from the earliest childhood memory. *Journal of Personality Assessment, 46*, 380–390.

Bruhn, A. R., & Tobey, L. H. (2018). *Early memories and dangerousness: A clinical approach*. Manuscript in preparation.

Burton, S., & Lynn, C. (2017). *Becoming Ms. Burton*. New York: New Press.

Chess, S. (1951). Utilization of childhood memories in psychoanalytic theory. *Journal of Child Psychiatry, 2*, 187–193.

Colegrove, F. (1899). Individual memories. *American Journal of Psychology, 10*, 228–255.

Davidow, S., & Bruhn, A. R. (1990). Earliest memories and the dynamics of delinquency: A replication study. *Journal of Personality Assessment, 54*, 601–616.

DeMuth, P., & Bruhn, A. R. (1997). The use of the Early Memories Procedure in a psychotherapy group of substance abusers. *International Journal of Offender Therapy and Comparative Criminology, 41*, 24–35.

Doidge, N. (2007). *The brain that changes itself: Stories of personal triumph from brain science*. New York: Viking.

Estrade, P. (2008). *You are what you remember* (L. Brumer, Trans.). Philadelphia, PA: Perseus.

Exner, J. E., Jr. (1974). *The Rorschach: A comprehensive system*. New York: Wiley.

Freud, S. (1899/1913). *The interpretation of dreams* (A.A. Brill, Trans.). New York: Macmillan.

Freud, S. (1917/1955). Screen memories. In J. Strachey (Ed. & Trans.), *The standard edition of the complete works of Sigmund Freud* (Vol 17). London: Hogarth Press.

Haley, J. (1973/1986). *Uncommon therapy: The psychiatric techniques of Milton H. Erickson, M.D.* New York: Norton.

Hartmann, H. (1958). *Ego psychology and the problem of adaptation*. New York: International Universities Press.

Hartmann, H. (1964). *Essays on ego psychology*. New York: International Universities Press.

Henri, V., & Henri, C. (1898). Earliest recollections. *Popular Science Monthly, 53*, 109–115.

Howe, M. L. (2000). *The fate of early memories: Developmental science and the retention of childhood experiences*. Washington, DC: American Psychological Association.

James, W. (1890). *The principles of psychology* (2 vols). New York: Henry Holt & Co.

120 References

Jung, C. (1963). *Memories, dreams, and reflections.* New York: Random House.

Kandel, E. R. (2006). *In search of memory: The emergence of a new science of mind.* New York: Norton.

Karson, M. (2006). *Using early memories in psychotherapy.* Lanham, MD: Jason Aronson.

Kotre, J. (1995). *White gloves: How we create ourselves through memory.* New

Projective Techniques and Personality Assessment, 32, 302–316.

Mayman, M. (1984). Psychoanalytic study of the self-organization with psychological tests. In F. Schechman & W. H. Smith (Eds.), *Diagnostic understanding and treatment planning: The elusive connection* (pp. 141–156). New York: Wiley.

Miles, C. (1893). A study of individual memories. *American Journal of Psychology, 6,* 534–558.

Millon, T. (2006). *MCMI-III manual (Millon Clinical Multiaxial Inventory-III).* Bloomington, MN: NCS Pearson.

Mollon, P. (2002). *Remembering trauma: A psychotherapist's guide to memory and illusion* (second edition). Philadelphia, PA: Whurr Publishers.

Mosak, H. H. (1958). Early recollection as a projective technique. *Journal of Projective Techniques, 22,* 303–311.

Mosak, H. H., & Di Pietro, R. (2006). *Early recollections: Interpretative method and application.* New York: Routledge.

Munroe, R.L. (1955). *Schools of psychoanalytic thought.* New York: Dryden.

Neisser, U. (1982). *Memory observed: Remembering in natural contexts.* San Francisco, CA: Freeman.

Olson, H. A. (1979). *Early recollections: Their use in diagnosis and psychotherapy.* Springfield, IL: Charles C. Thomas.

Parnell, L. (2007). *A therapist's guide to EMDR: Tools and techniques for successful treatment.* New York: Norton.

Pepper, S. C. (1942). *World hypotheses: A study in evidence.* Berkeley, CA: University of California Press.

Piaget, J. (1977). *The development of thought: Equilibration of cognitive structures* (A. Rosin, Trans.). Oxford: Viking.

References 121

Richards, H. J. (1993). *Therapy of the substance abuse syndromes.* New York: Jason Aronson.

Richards, H. J., Bruhn, A. R., Lucente, S. W., & Casey, J. O. (2015). Reliability of the comprehensive Scoring System with the Early Memories Procedure. *Sensoria: A Journal of Mind, Brain & Culture, 10* (2), 14–22.

Ross, B. M. (1991). *Remembering the personal past: Descriptions of autobiographical memory.* New York: Oxford University Press.

Rubin, D. (1986). *Autobiographical memory.* New York: Cambridge University Press.

Saul, L. J., Snyder, T. R., & Sheppard, E. (1956). On earliest memories. *Psychoanalytic Quarterly, 25,* 228–237.

Schiffman, H. (1998). Milton Erickson: Scientist, hypnotist, healer. In G. A. Kimble & M. Wertheimer (Eds.), *Portraits of pioneers in psychology* (Vol. 3, pp. 180–195). Washington, DC: American Psychological Association.

Shapiro, F. (1989). Eye movement desensitization: A new treatment for posttraumatic stress disorder. *Journal of Behavior Therapy and Experimental Psychiatry, 20,* 211–217.

Shapiro, F. (1999). Does EMDR work? And if so, why? A critical review of controlled outcome and dismantling research. *Journal of Anxiety Disorders, 13,* 5–33.

Singer, J. A., & Salovey, P. (1993). *The remembered self: Emotion and memory in personality.* New York: Free Press.

Theiler, S. (2009). *Early memories: Theory, research, and practice: Accessing essential meaning in counseling.* Saarbrücken: VDM Verlag Dr. Müller.

Tobey, L. H., & Bruhn, A. R. (1992). Early memories and the criminally dangerous. *Journal of Personality Assessment, 59,* 137–152.

Waldfogel, S. (1948). The frequency and affective character of childhood memories. *Psychological Monographs, 62,* (4).

Index

physical 41, 62, 63–64, 67–68, 95, 109–110, 112–113, 116; psychosis 17n9; undisclosed 24, 33–35, 56; women prison inmates 15, 82; *see also* child molestation
Achenbach, T. M. 18
Acklin, M. W. 8
action-oriented therapy 67
Adler, Alfred 1, 6, 9, 10, 22, 25n1, 45
Adlerian theory 1, 5, 6, 13, 25n2, 39, 100
affective quality 45
affective tone 41n2
aggression 87, 113
alcohol abuse 58, 60–61; case study 58, 106–107, 109–111, 113–114; memories related to alcohol 60, 76n1; parental 62; prison inmates 93n2; *see also* substance abuse
anger 28, 98, 100, 112
anger management 12, 93
Ansbacher, H. & R. 6, 9, 13
anxiety 61–62, 66, 73, 98; case study 111, 113; EMDR 29; fear of abandonment 59; hemp-oil drops 105; PTSD client 27; "stuckness" 100
assessment 1, 2–3, 21, 32–33, 45, 75; *see also* Early Memories Procedure

organization of 42n4; retention of experience in 94–97, 98; selected publications on 8–13; taxonomy of 77–78, 81; theory of 29; writing down memories 53–54; *see also* early memories; Early Memories Procedure; memories

Baldwin, James 58
Bartlett, F. C. 9, 11
Beck, Aaron 10
behaviorism 18
Bellow, S. 10
Bergson, H. 1, 26, 77; forgetting 6; utility principle 3, 4, 6, 16n6, 38, 40, 96
Bibb, J. L. 8
Binder, J. L. 9
bipolar disorder 58, 107, 111
bizarre material 87, 119
bonding 44, 83, 84, 87
borderline personality disorder 107, 111, 112
Boyer, P. 8
brain maturation 4, 52
Bruhn, Arnold R.: Cognitive-Perceptual theory 7, 10, 11, 21, 29; EMP 20–21, 22, 40; injury memories 93n1; memory networks

29; prison inmates 79, 83–84, 85, 88–89, 91–92, 97–99; selected publications 8–13
Burton, S. 82

case study 58, 106–114
Casey, J. O. 79
CEMSS *see* Comprehensive Early Memories Scoring System
CEMSS-R *see* Comprehensive Early Memories Scoring System—Revised
change 3–4, 58, 61, 95–96, 100
child molestation 3, 14–15, 16n5; client's view as positive experience 20, 48–49; psychosis 17n9; undisclosed 22, 33–35, 56; women prison inmates 15, 82; *see also* abuse
Child Protective Services (CPS) 14–15
clarity 45, 78, 97
clearest memories 21, 22, 43n7; affective quality 45, 46; case study 112; focus on 55; illness 80; "load-bearing memories" 47, 75; negative 48; principle of attraction 40; themes 79
cognitive change 3, 4
Cognitive-Perceptual (CP) theory 5, 19, 21, 29, 97; compared with psychoanalytic theory 42n4; early memories 7; selected publications 6, 9, 10, 11
cognitive theory 10
Colegrove, F. 4, 8
Comprehensive Early Memories Scoring System (CEMSS) 9, 80
Comprehensive Early Memories Scoring System—Revised (CEMSS-R) 11, 12, 44, 46, 78–80, 87, 93n1, 113, 115–119
context 39
cooperative play 87, 117
criminals *see* prison inmates
cultural issues 80–81

dangerousness 8, 11–12, 37–39
Davidow, S. 10
delinquency 8, 10
DeMuth, Peter 51, 83–84, 85, 91–92, 97–99
depression 8, 61–62, 75; case study 111, 114; EMP 22; memories associated with 2; PTSD client 27; "stuckness" 100; thinking errors 10

Di Pietro, R. 13
diagnosis 111
Diagnostic and Statistical Manual of Mental Disorders (DSM) 18, 107
directed memories 6, 20, 46, 77–79, 97
divorce 33, 34, 106
Doidge, N. 52
dreams 8, 19, 80, 99
DSM see Diagnostic and Statistical Manual of Mental Disorders

early memories 1, 2–3; Adlerian theory 1, 47; Cognitive-Perceptual theory 7; earliest memories 15n4, 20, 23n1, 40, 47–48, 62; importance of 68; perceptographs 36; psychological variables 8; selected publications on 8–13; theories of 6, 29; *see also* autobiographical memory; memories
Early Memories Aggressiveness Potential Score System (EMAPSS) 11–12
The Early Memories Procedure (EMP) 2–3, 5, 14–15, 19–22, 46; case examples 62, 63, 68–69, 70, 106–107, 110, 111–114; false memories 16n5; forgetting 7; Franklin 41, 95; introducing the 55–56; "load-bearing memories" 47, 75; memories linked by association 39–40; principle of attraction 40; prison inmates 83–84, 85, 92, 98; PTSD client 27–29; recurring events 97; relationships 56–57; risk reduction 32; scoring of memories 79; selected publications 10, 11, 13; training 99; traumatic memories 48; undisclosed abuse 33–35, 56; writing down memories 53–54
ego-psychology 5, 6, 29
Eisenhower, Dwight David 10, 13
Eliot, George 100
EMAPSS *see* Early Memories Aggressiveness Potential Score System
EMDR *see* eye movement desensitization and reprocessing
emotions 12; *see also* negative affect; positive affect
EMP *see* Early Memories Procedure
empathy 83
empowerment 34, 85, 86, 92, 97–98

124 *Index*

Erickson, Milton 22–23, 72–73, 109
  see also "February Man"
Estrade, P. 6, 13
Exner's Comprehensive System 78
expectations 5, 32; negative 37, 39, 39–40, 45, 79; prison inmates 8

dreams 8, 99; on Goethe 9; repressed memories 40, 46, 9; self-analysis 68; unconscious motivation 67; wishes 37
Freudian theory 1, 5, 6, 8, 29

Gandhi, Mahatma 13
gaps in early life experiences 72–73
gender identification memories 78
giftedness 87, 94, 117
Goethe, Johann 9
grief 87, 89
group identification memories 77, 78
group treatment 83, 84, 85, 99

Haley, J. 22–23, 73
healing 84
hemp-oil drops 110
Henri, V. & C. 8
Hippocratic oath 32
history 11, 24–26, 77
hospitalization memories 12, 79, 80, 87, 115
Howe, M. L. 12

ideographic aspects 12
illness memories 12, 79–80, 87, 98–99, 115; *see also* medical problems
immune system 51, 98
information processing 4

injury memories 12, 79–80, 86, 87, 93n1, 115
insight-oriented therapy 14, 19, 27, 30, 56, 99; EMP 20–21, 54; prison inmates 82, 85, 86, 90, 97–98; *see also* therapy

110; transformational moments 58
locus of control 8, 20
Loftus, E. 8, 16n5
loss 2, 87, 91, 115
Lucas, Jerry 7
Lucente, S. W. 79
Lynn, C. 82

maladjustment 8
marital issues 33, 106
mastery: CEMSS-R themes 44, 46, 79, 87, 113, 116, 117; cultural values 80
maturation 4
Mayman, M. 9
medical problems 50, 51, 52n1, 98–100; *see also* illness memories
medication 28, 106, 107, 110
Meier, Golda 10, 13
memories: Adler's view of 6; alcohol-related 60, 76n1; alternative views of 26; dysfunctional 72; in fiction 24; as history and metaphor 24–25; interpretation of 25; linked by association 39–40; Mosak on 100; negative 26, 37–40, 41n2, 46, 95, 112; positive 37, 38, 41n2, 112; power to effect change 61; prison inmates 12, 51, 82–93, 97–98, 99; retention of 94–97, 99; taxonomy of 77–79, 81; themes 44,

46, 78–80, 87, 94, 97, 115–119; traumatic 2, 14, 17n9, 48, 58, 85, 86–89; "unfinished business" 29; writing down 53–54; *see also* autobiographical memory; clearest memories; early memories; The Early Memories Procedure
memory language system 26
memory networks 29
Merkel, Angela 43n8
metaphors, memories as 24–25
Miles, C. 8
Millon, T. 18
mistakes 26
Mollon, P. 48
mood 5, 80
Mosak, H. H. 13, 100
motivation 67
Muir, John 13
Munroe, Ruth 23n1, 47

National Institute of Drug Abuse (NIDA) 12, 79, 87, 90–93, 96, 97–98, 99, 120–121
needs 37–39, 40, 42n4, 44, 45, 70, 87, 94, 97, 112
negative affect 6, 26, 37–40, 41n2, 44; case study 112; CEMSS-R themes 115; clearest memories 43n7, 45, 46, 48; issues requiring resolution 97, 98; précis 39–40, 79; prison inmates 86; repeated negative experiences 95; taxonomy of memory variables 77–78
Neisser, U. 9, 10, 11
neurons 52
NIDA *see* National Institute of Drug Abuse
Nixon, Richard 13

Olson, H. A. 9, 23n1

Parnell, L. 29
Pepper, S. C. 42n4
perception 9, 11, 77
perceptographs 36, 39, 40, 41n1, 46, 97, 113
personality 4–5, 46; brain maturation 4; change 3; CP theory 11, 20; "lost" 15n2; personality assessment 1, 5, 12, 100; reorganization of 75; theory of 1, 5, 15n3
personality disorders 107, 111
photographic memory 7, 16n7

physical abuse 41, 62, 63–64, 66–67, 95, 107–110, 112–113, 116; *see also* abuse
Piaget, J. 4
positive affect 6, 41n2, 76n1; case study 112; clearest memories 43n7, 45; issues requiring resolution 98; needs 37, 39, 40, 44, 79, 97; prison inmates 86, 87; retention of experience in memory 95; taxonomy of memory variables 77–79
post-traumatic stress disorder (PTSD) 27–28, 29, 37, 111
précis method 39–40, 42n6, 79
prison inmates 3, 12, 15, 51, 79, 82–93, 96, 97–98, 99, 120–121
professional responsibility 35
projective tests 47
psychic energy 1, 42n4, 43n7, 45, 78, 97
psychoanalysis 6, 42n4
psychopathology 18
psychosis 17n9, 87, 119
PTSD *see* post-traumatic stress disorder
punishment 48, 63; CEMSS-R themes 46, 87, 113, 116; physical 66–67, 110, 112–113; recurring events 97
Putin, Vladimir 43n8

recidivism 12, 90–93, 98, 99, 120–121
Reiser, M. F. 9
rejection 38, 87, 112, 113, 116
relationships 56–57, 68, 69–70; abusive 63–64; EMP 21; mistrust in 71, 72
repeated events 77, 78, 95, 97
repressed memories 1, 8, 19, 40, 46, 99
repression 8, 42n4, 46
reverse-engineering 3, 39, 40, 44, 97
Richards, Henry 12, 79, 82–83, 89–91
Romantic Relationships Procedure (RRP) 10, 19, 57
Rorschach scoring system 77, 79
Ross, B. M. 11
RRP *see* Romantic Relationships Procedure
Rubin, D. 10
rule breaking 87, 118

Salovey, P. 12
sarcoidosis 50–51, 98

126 Index

Saul, L. J. 47–48
schemas 42n4
Schiffman, Harold 9, 20, 23n4, 24
security 44
self-analysis 66, 68, 75
self-awareness 3, 19, 20–21

49, 77–78, 97
stories 44, 45
strategic therapies 22–23
stress 28, 98–99
"stuckness" 38, 100
style of life 47
substance abuse 70, 72; case study 58,
    106, 110; prison inmates 12, 79,
    82, 88–89, 91, 120–121
succorance 87, 117

taxonomies 77–78, 81
templates 23, 26, 68, 75
Theiler, S. 8, 13

themes 44, 46, 78–80, 87, 94, 97,
    115–119
Therapeutic Community treatment
    89–91, 92, 98
therapy: action-oriented 67; active
    approach to 19, 58; fear of

Trump, Donald 43n8
trust 14, 39, 66, 72, 98; case study
    109, 110; CEMSS-R themes 44, 87,
    116; loss of 38

"unfinished business" 29
utility, principle of 3, 4, 6, 16n6, 38,
    40, 96

violent prisoners 91–92

Waldfogel, S. 9
women prison inmates 3, 12, 15, 51,
    79, 82–93, 96, 97–98, 99, 120–121